Step Forward supports learners as they work to meet the *English Language Proficiency Standards for Adult Education* (ELPS) and the *College and Career Readiness Standards for Adult Education* (CCR). See *Step Forward's* **Teacher Resource Center** for step-by-step lesson plans that list the level-specific ELP and CCR standards, and for other detailed correlations.

LANGUAGE STRATEGIES		COLLEGE & CAREER READINESS	
Reading & Writing	**Listening & Speaking**	**Critical Thinking**	**Collaboration**
■ Write names ■ Read and write numbers 1–100 ■ Write phone numbers ■ Write addresses	**Conversation** ■ Say and spell names	**Critical thinking** ■ Process instructions	■ Understands teamwork and works with others
■ Read a school registration form ■ Complete a form ■ Write sentences about personal information ■ Read about different methods of studying English **Reading strategy** ■ Capital letters in names **Writing strategy** ■ Previewing titles	**Conversation** ■ Common greetings and introductions ■ Talk about people and things in the classroom **Focused Listening** ■ Follow directions ■ Introduce people **Pronunciation** ■ Practice using contractions	**Critical thinking** ■ Differentiate elements of personal information ■ Identify effective language-learning habits ■ Analyze personal language-learning goals **Problem solving** ■ Determine appropriate responses to greetings and introductions	■ Locate information ■ Communicate information
■ Read basic information about a student ■ Write sentences with personal information ■ Read a text on where people are from in the U.S. ■ Interpret and make a graph about people's origins **Writing strategy** ■ Using commas in dates **Reading strategy** ■ Using footnotes	**Conversation** ■ Give and ask about personal information ■ Ask for help at work **Focused Listening** ■ Listen in order to complete a registration form ■ Listen in order to determine someone's identity **Pronunciation** ■ Practice the differences in *Miss, Mrs., Mr.,* and *Ms.*	**Critical thinking** ■ Interpret clock times and dates ■ Interpret a calendar ■ Analyze population statistics ■ Interpret graphs **Problem solving** ■ Determine how to solve problems and ask for help in the classroom	■ Think critically ■ Locate information ■ Ask for help
■ Read and write about a family member or friend ■ Read about small and large families ■ Use chart information to understand a reading ■ Make a chart with classroom information **Writing strategy** ■ Indenting paragraphs **Reading strategy** ■ Interpreting pie chart percentages	**Conversation** ■ Ask and answer questions about classmates ■ Talk about times and dates ■ Practice making outgoing voicemail messages **Focused Listening** ■ Listen for information about people, dates, and times **Pronunciation** ■ Practice with endings on ordinal numbers	**Critical thinking** ■ Compare family sizes ■ Interpret information in a chart **Problem solving** ■ Find and correct an error on a document	■ Locate information ■ Communicate verbally ■ Analyze information ■ Communicate information

SECOND EDITION

STEP FORWARD

STANDARDS-BASED LANGUAGE LEARNING FOR WORK AND ACADEMIC READINESS

1

SERIES DIRECTOR
Jayme Adelson-Goldstein

Jenni Currie Santamaria

OXFORD
UNIVERSITY PRESS

TABLE OF CONTENTS

Grammar charts pages 172-178

LANGUAGE STRATEGIES		COLLEGE & CAREER READINESS	
Reading & Writing	**Listening & Speaking**	**Critical Thinking**	**Collaboration**
■ Read about shopping at a mall ■ Write about shopping ■ Read an article about credit and debit cards **Reading strategy** ■ Using hyperlinks in website articles **Writing strategy** ■ Using *but* to connect sentences	**Conversation** ■ Talk about things that are nearby or far away ■ Request specific clothing from a salesperson **Focused Listening** ■ Listen for sizing and clothing prices **Pronunciation** ■ Differentiate between *-teen* and *-ty* numbers	**Critical thinking** ■ Compare and contrast clothing ■ Apply concept of credit card interest **Problem solving** ■ Determine how to resolve ATM problems	■ Listen actively ■ Communicate verbally ■ Analyze information ■ Manage money
■ Read and write about food shopping ■ Read a supermarket ad ■ Write a shopping list ■ Read a menu ■ Read about healthy food ■ Read food labels ■ Write questions with *How often* **Reading strategy** ■ Using *because* to answer the question *Why?* **Writing strategy** ■ Using commas in a list	**Conversation** ■ Talk about food shopping ■ Ask and answer questions about your classmates' routines ■ Ordering food in a restaurant ■ Confirming information **Focused Listening** ■ Listen in order to complete food orders **Pronunciation** ■ Differentiating between questions and answers	**Critical thinking** ■ Interpret items on a menu ■ Analyze healthy and unhealthy eating habits **Problem solving** ■ Analyze and negotiate good eating habits for family members	■ Respond to customer needs ■ Communicate information ■ Use information
■ Read and write about a doctor's appointment ■ Write a paragraph about being healthy ■ Read an article about ways to be healthy ■ Read directions and warnings on medicine labels **Reading strategy** ■ Using headings in an article **Writing strategy** ■ Using words like *then* and *after that*	**Conversation** ■ Ask and answer questions with *have to* ■ Ask and answer questions about your day ■ Practice making an appointment **Focused Listening** ■ Listen for medical advice ■ listen for information to complete an appointment card **Pronunciation** ■ Differentiating between *have* and *have to*	**Critical thinking** ■ Analyze and compare medical advice ■ Classify obligations by level of importance ■ Assess a schedule to make appointments ■ Interpret warnings on medical labels **Problem solving** ■ Determine how to handle obligations when sick	■ Communicate information ■ Analyze information ■ Manage time

LANGUAGE STRATEGIES		COLLEGE & CAREER READINESS	
Reading & Writing	**Listening & Speaking**	**Critical Thinking**	**Collaboration**
■ Read job listings ■ Read and write an email to an employer about a job ■ Write about work histories ■ Read an article about what makes a great employee ■ Read a chart about why some employees don't succeed **Reading strategy** ■ Using an example in a text **Writing strategy** ■ Placing personal information in an email	**Conversation** ■ Ask and answer *yes/no* questions ■ Ask and answer questions about the past ■ Ask and answer interview questions **Focused Listening** ■ Listen for information about a person's work history **Pronunciation** ■ Differentiating *can* and *can't*	**Critical thinking** ■ Interpret help-wanted ads ■ Analyze and describe personal work experience **Problem solving** ■ Compare jobs based on salary and hours	■ Communicate information ■ Think critically ■ Use information
■ Read about safe and dangerous behavior ■ Write about personal safety habits ■ Write classroom rules ■ Read an article about car safety ■ Read a chart about teen car accidents **Reading strategy** ■ Using frequency adverbs in a text **Writing strategy** ■ Using *however* and *but* when writing	**Conversation** ■ Ask and answer information questions with *should* ■ Practice making 911 calls ■ Describe emergencies ■ Prepare for emergencies **Focused Listening** ■ Listen for information about a safety checklist ■ Listen for emergency information **Pronunciation** ■ Differentiating *should* and *shouldn't*	**Critical thinking** ■ Interpret traffic signs ■ Classify behavior as safe or unsafe ■ Classify language learning habits as positive or negative ■ Identify emergencies to a 911 operator ■ Analyze a pie chart of accident data **Problem solving** ■ Determine appropriate behavior following an accident	■ Communicate information ■ Use information ■ Solve problems ■ Understand teamwork and work with others
■ Read about a trip to a baseball game ■ Write about a leisure activity ■ Read a college catalog ■ Read an article about planning the future **Reading strategy** ■ Understanding the purpose of an article **Writing strategy** ■ Using concluding sentences	**Conversation** ■ Talk about future plans with classmates ■ Discuss personal goals and plans ■ Practice encouraging others **Pronunciation** ■ Differentiating formal and relaxed pronunciation	**Critical thinking** ■ Classify leisure activities by season ■ Assess information in a college course catalog ■ Create a flowchart **Problem solving** ■ Determine how to modify plans due to bad weather	■ Think critically ■ Manage time ■ Plan and organize

WELCOME TO THE SECOND EDITION OF *STEP FORWARD*!

"What's new?" is a question that often greets the arrival of a second edition, but let's start with the similarities between *Step Forward Second Edition* and its predecessor. This edition retains the original's effective instructional practices for teaching adult English language learners, such as focusing on learner outcomes, learner-centered lessons, thematic four-skill integration with associated vocabulary, direct instruction of grammar and pronunciation, focused listening, and sourced texts. It also preserves the instructional flexibility that allows it to be used in classes that meet twice a week, and those that meet every day. Perhaps most significantly, this edition continues to provide the differentiation support for teachers in multilevel settings.

The *College and Career Readiness Standards for Adult Education* (Pimentel, 2013) and the 2016 *English Language Proficiency Standards* echo the research by ACT, Parrish and Johnson, Wrigley, and others linking critical thinking skills, academic language, and language strategies to learners' academic success and employability. Rigorous language instruction is key to accelerating our learners' transition into family-sustaining jobs, civic engagement, and/or post-secondary education. *Step Forward Second Edition* has integrated civic, college, and career readiness skills in every lesson. Each *Step Forward* author considered adult learners' time constraints while crafting lessons that flow from objective to outcome, encouraging and challenging learners with relevant tasks that ensure their growth.

STEP FORWARD KEY CONCEPTS

Our learners' varied proficiency levels, educational backgrounds, goals, and interests make the English language classroom a remarkable place. They also create some instructional challenges. To ensure that your learners leave class having made progress toward their language and life goals, these key concepts underpin the *Step Forward* curriculum.

Effective instruction…

▸ acknowledges and makes use of learners' prior knowledge and critical thinking skills.

▸ helps learners develop the language that allows them to demonstrate their 21st century skills.

▸ contextualizes lessons to support learners' workplace, career, and civic goals.

▸ ensures that each lesson's learning objectives, instructions, and tasks are clear.

▸ differentiates instruction in order to accommodate learners at varying proficiency levels within the same class.

▸ provides informational text (including graphs, charts, and images) that builds and expands learners' knowledge.

STEP FORWARD COMPONENTS

Each level of *Step Forward* correlates to *The Oxford Picture Dictionary*. Each *Step Forward* level includes the following components:

Step Forward Student Book
Twelve thematic units focusing on everyday adult topics, each with six lessons integrating communication, workplace, and academic skills, along with language strategies for accuracy and fluency.

Step Forward Audio Program
The recorded vocabulary, focused listening, conversations, pronunciation, and reading materials from the *Step Forward* Student Book.

Step Forward Workbook
Practice exercises for independent work in the classroom or as homework, as well as "Do the Math" sections.

Step Forward Teacher Resource Center
An online collection of downloadable resources that support the *Step Forward* program. The *Step Forward* Teacher Resource Center contains the following components:

• *Step Forward* Lesson Plans: an instructional planning resource with detailed, step-by-step lesson plans featuring multilevel teaching strategies and teaching tips

• *Step Forward* Multilevel Activities: over 100 communicative practice activities and 72 picture cards; lesson materials that work equally well in single-level or multilevel settings

• *Step Forward* Multilevel Grammar Exercises: multilevel grammar practice for the structures presented in the *Step Forward* Student Book

• *Step Forward* Testing Program: tests for every unit in the *Step Forward* Student Book

• *Step Forward* Literacy Reproducible Activities: literacy activities that correspond to the *Step Forward Introductory Level* Student Book, intended to support pre-beginning or semi-literate level learners

• Correlations: correlations to national standards, including the *College and Career Readiness Standards* and the *English Language Proficiency Standards*

• *Step Forward* Answer Keys and Audio Scripts for the *Step Forward* Student Book and Workbook

Step Forward Classroom Presentation Tool
On-screen *Step Forward* Student Book pages, including audio at point of use and whole-class interactive activities, transform each Student Book into a media-rich classroom presentation tool in order to maximize-heads up learning. The intuitive, book-on-screen design helps teachers navigate easily from page to page.

I know I speak for the authors and the entire *Step Forward* publishing team when I say it's a privilege to serve you and your learners.

Jayme Adelson-Goldstein

Jayme Adelson-Goldstein, Series Director

WELCOME, LEARNERS!

Learning English is a challenge. *Step Forward* can help. Here are some ideas to try.

STUDY THE LISTS, CHARTS, AND NOTES
They give you information about English.

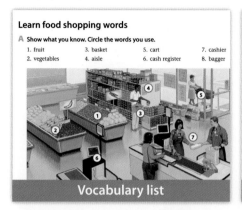

Vocabulary list

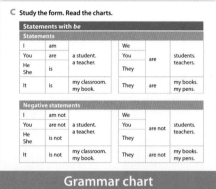

Grammar chart

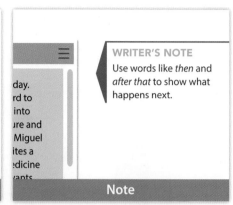

WRITER'S NOTE
Use words like *then* and *after that* to show what happens next.

Note

BE BRAVE IN CLASS
Practice helps you use English.

ASK QUESTIONS
Questions help you understand.

COLLABORATE
Work with your classmates, and study alone too.

Work with a partner

Work with a team

Work alone

Welcome **xi**

The First Step

1 Spell your name

A Listen and look at the pictures.

1-02

① Point to a letter.

② Say your name.
Tom

③ Spell your name.
T-O-M

B Listen and repeat.

1-03

The Alphabet

A	B	C	D	E	F	G	H	I	J	K	L	M
a	b	c	d	e	f	g	h	i	j	k	l	m

N	O	P	Q	R	S	T	U	V	W	X	Y	Z
n	o	p	q	r	s	t	u	v	w	x	y	z

C Listen and spell the names.

1-04

1. M _a_ _r_ _i_ _a_
2. L ____ ____
3. T ____ ____

4. R ____ b ____ ____ ____ a
5. K ____ m a ____
6. ____ a ____ i ____

D Work with 2–3 classmates. Say and spell your name.

A: I'm Jack.
B: Please spell that.
A: J-A-C-K

A: I'm Carmen.
B: Excuse me? I don't understand.
A: I'm Carmen. C-A-R-M-E-N.

2 Learn numbers 1–20

🔊 1-05 **A** Listen and say the numbers.

1 one	**2** two	**3** three	**4** four	**5** five
6 six	**7** seven	**8** eight	**9** nine	**10** ten
11 eleven	**12** twelve	**13** thirteen	**14** fourteen	**15** fifteen
16 sixteen	**17** seventeen	**18** eighteen	**19** nineteen	**20** twenty

NEED HELP?

0 = zero

You can say "O" instead of "zero" in phone numbers and addresses.

B Work with a partner. Partner A: Say a phone number. Partner B: Listen and write the phone number.

1. (213) 555-3611
2. (908) 555-1468
3. (608) 555-1284
4. (714) 555-9502
5. (698) 555-0224
6. (473) 555-5892

phone number

C Work with a partner. Partner A: Say an address. Partner B: Listen and write the address.

1. 1711 G Street
2. 2098 B Street
3. 613 K Street
4. 13458 Q Street
5. 8721 J Street
6. 909 G Street

address

3 Learn more numbers

🔊 1-06 **A** Listen and count from 20 to 30.

20   21   22   23   24   25   26   27   28   29   30

🔊 1-07 **B** Listen and count by tens.

10 ten	**20** twenty	**30** thirty	**40** fourty	**50** fifty
60 sixty	**70** seventy	**80** eighty	**90** ninety	**100** one hundred

🔊 1-08 **C** Listen and write the numbers.

1. _____
2. _____
3. _____
4. _____
5. _____
6. _____
7. _____
8. _____

UNIT

1 Say Hello

A LOOK AT
- The classroom
- Statements with *be*
- Introducing people

LESSON 1 VOCABULARY

1 Learn classroom directions

A Show what you know. Circle the words you use.

1. listen to	3. say	5. open	7. sit down
2. point to	4. repeat	6. close	8. stand up

 B Listen and look at the pictures.
1-09

 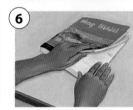  

 C Listen and repeat the words from 1A.
1-10

D Look at the pictures. Complete the sentences. Use the words in the box.

Point	Sit	Say	Close	Listen to	Stand	~~Open~~	Repeat

1. _Open_ the notebook.
2. _____ the letter D.
3. _____ the book, please.
4. _____ to the letter B.

5. _____ down, please.
6. _____ up, please.
7. _____ the letter C.
8. _____ the letter A.

E Read your sentences to a partner. Then listen to your partner and follow the directions.

2 Talk about a classroom

A Work in a team. Match the words with the picture. Look up new words in the dictionary.

_a_ board	____ chair	____ desk	____ notebook	____ student
____ book	____ clock	____ dictionary	____ pen	____ teacher

1-11

B Listen and check your answers. Then practice the words with a partner.

C Complete the chart. Then say the words with a partner.

Singular (1)	Plural (2, 3, 4…)
a desk	desks
a chair	
a teacher	
	boards
	notebooks

GRAMMAR NOTE

a yellow pencil   two yellow pencils

D Work with a partner. Listen to your partner read the sentences. Follow the directions.

1. Point to a chair.
2. Please stand up.
3. Say your name.
4. Sit down, please.
5. Open your notebook.
6. Close your book.

▶▶ **TEST YOURSELF**

Make a chart like this one. Close your book.
Write three words in each column.

Directions	Things or people

1 Prepare to write

A Look at the picture and the form. Spell Jim's last name.

SCHOOL REGISTRATION FORM

Name:

1. _____ Jim Santos _____
   (first) (last)

Address:

2. _____ 27 Lima Street, Apt. 3 _____
   (street)
   _____ Dallas, Texas 75202 _____
   (city) (state) (zip code)

Telephone:

3. _____ (214) 555-1204 _____
   (area code)

Email:

4. _____ Jsantos@work.net _____

Signature:

5. _____ Jim Santos _____

B Look at the pictures in 1A. Listen. What's on line 5?
1-12

C Listen and read the sentences.
1-13

1. Tell me your first name. Please spell your last name.

2. Complete the form. Please print your address.

3. Write your telephone number with the area code. Then write your email address.

4. Sign your name on line five.

5. Please give me the form. Welcome to school.

D Check your understanding. Match the numbers with the letters.

_b_ 1. tell   a. J-I-M.

____ 2. spell   b. Jim

____ 3. print   c. *Jim Santos*

____ 4. sign   d. Jim Santos

E Listen. Look at the student ID card. Circle *a* or *b*.
1-14

1. a. Elm Street   (b.) Ramirez

2. a. 555-1242   b. 16

3. a. (323)   b. 90011

4. a. 16 Elm Street   b. joseram@123.net

5. a. Jose   b. Ramirez

6. a. Los Angeles   b. *Jose Ramirez*

Jose Ramirez
16 Elm Street
Los Angeles, CA 90011
(323) 555-1242
email: joseram@123.net

Jose Ramirez

2 Plan

A Listen and follow the directions. Use your own information.

1. _____   4. _____

2. _____   5. _____

3. _____   6. _____

B Work with a partner. Practice the conversation. Use your own information.

A: Tell me your first name.   A: Tell me your last name.

B: Maria.   B: Gonzalez.

A: Please spell that for me.   A: Please spell that for me.

B: M-A-R-I-A.   B: G-O-N-Z-A-L-E-Z.

3 Write

A Complete the form. Use your own information.

1. Name: _____
         (first)   (last)

2. Telephone: (_____) _____
              (area code)

3. Address: _____

   _____

4. Signature: _____

> **WRITER'S NOTE**
> Use capital letters in names:
>
> **M**aria
>
> **E**lm Street

B Read your form to a partner.

▶ TEST YOURSELF

Complete the following sentences. Share your responses with your teacher.

1. After this writing lesson, I can…
2. I need more help with…

1 Explore the verb *be*: meaning and form

A **Look at the pictures. Read the sentences. Count the students in each picture.**

My Class

| I am a student. | He is my teacher. | She is my partner. | They are my classmates. | We are a group. | It is my classroom. |

B **Work with the grammar. Look at the sentences in 1A. Circle *am*, *is*, and *are*. Why do some sentences have *is*?**

C **Study the form. Read the charts.**

Statements with *be*					
Statements					
I	am	a student. a teacher.	We	are	students. teachers.
You	are	a student. a teacher.	You	are	students. teachers.
He She	is	a student. a teacher.	They	are	students. teachers.
It	is	my classroom. my book.	They	are	my books. my pens.

Negative statements					
I	am not	a student. a teacher.	We	are not	students. teachers.
You	are not	a student. a teacher.	You	are not	students. teachers.
He She	is not	a student. a teacher.	They	are not	students. teachers.
It	is not	my classroom. my book.	They	are not	my books. my pens.

D **Work with a partner. Look at the charts in 1C. Make sentences. Take turns.**

I am a student.   *You are a student.*

2 Practice: statements with the verb *be*

A Listen and repeat the words.

1-16

1. pencils
2. a teacher
3. a new student
4. a computer
5. a piece of paper
6. an eraser
7. a door
8. windows
9. a backpack
10. a wastebasket

B Look at the pictures in 2A. Circle the correct answer.

1. They ((are) / is) pencils.
2. She (is / are) a teacher.
3. (He is / They are) a new student.
4. It (is / am) a computer. It (is / is not) a pen.
5. (It is / He is) a piece of paper.
6. (It is / They are) an eraser.
7. It (is / is not) a door. It (is / is not) a window.
8. (It is / They are) windows.
9. It (is / is not) a book. It (is / is not) a backpack.
10. It (is / are) a wastebasket. It (is / is not) a backpack.

C Work with a partner. Make sentences about the pictures.

A: *They are pencils.*
B: *It's a computer.*

GRAMMAR NOTE

a or an?

a pencil	an eraser
a street	an address
a book	an I.D. card

3 Practice contractions with *be*

A Study the form. Listen to the words. Notice the two ways to make negative contractions.

Contractions	
I am = I'm	I am not = I'm not
you are = you're	you are not = you're not / you aren't
he is = he's	he is not = he's not / he isn't
she is = she's	she is not = she's not / she isn't
it is = it's	it is not = it's not / it isn't
we are = we're	we are not = we're not / we aren't
they are = they're	they are not = they're not / they aren't

B Work with the grammar. Circle the correct words.

1. ((I'm) / They're) a student.
2. (She's / It's) a teacher.
3. (He's / It's) a pen.
4. (He's / I'm) my partner.

5. (It isn't / They aren't) my books.
6. He (isn't / aren't) a teacher.
7. (It's / We're) a computer.
8. (It isn't / She isn't) an eraser.

C Complete the sentences about the picture.

1. _____ pencil.
2. _____ books.
3. _____ teacher.
4. _____ chair.

It's a board.

D Talk about people and things in your classroom. Follow the directions.

Student A: Point to a person or thing in your classroom.

Student B: Say what the person or thing is. Use contractions.

A: It's a board.   **B:** They're books.

▶▶ TEST YOURSELF

Close your book. Write five sentences about your classroom. Read your sentences to a partner.

1 Listen to learn: meeting new people

A Listen and read the conversations. Does *Good evening* mean *hello* or *goodbye*?

1-18

B Match the greeting in column A to the response in column B.

_____ 1. What's your name?   a. Nice to meet you too.

_____ 2. Good evening.   b. See you later.

_____ 3. Goodbye.   c. I'm Li.

_____ 4. How are you?   d. Hello.

_____ 5. It's nice to meet you.   e. Fine, thanks.

2 Practice your pronunciation

A Read the sentences. Listen for the contractions.

1-19

No contraction	Contraction
What is your name?	What's your name?
I am Maria.	I'm Maria.
It is nice to meet you.	It's nice to meet you.

B Listen and check (✓) *no contraction* or *contraction*.

1-20

	1.	2.	3.	4.	5.
no contraction	✓				
contraction					

C Work with a partner. Say the sentences in 2A. Practice with and without contractions.

3 Introduce people

A Listen and read the conversation. Who is Ms. Simpson?

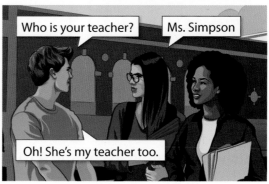

B Listen and circle *a* or *b*.

1. a. My name is Asha.
   b. This is my friend Sara.
2. a. Nice to meet you too.
   b. Yes, I'm Asha.

3. a. I'm Tim.
   b. Ms. Simpson.
4. a. Nice to meet you.
   b. Oh! She's my teacher too.

C Think about the grammar. Look at the conversation. Do we use *who* or *what* for questions about people?

D Study the grammar. Listen and repeat the questions and answers.

Information questions with *be*	
Questions with *what*	**Questions with *who***
What's your phone number? It's (213) 555-2535.	Who are you? I'm a student.
What are they? They're my books.	Who are they? They're my classmates.
What is it? It's my new computer.	Who is he? He's my teacher.

E Complete the questions. Then ask and answer the questions with a partner.

Dear Dalien

PARVEEN

1. _____ is it?

2. _____ is she?

3. _____ _____ they?

4 Make conversation: meeting new people

A Work with a partner. Make a new conversation.

A: Good _____ . I'm _____ .
What's your name?

B: My name is _____ .

A: Can you repeat that, please?

B: Yes. I'm _____ . It's nice to meet you, _____ .

A: Nice to meet you too.

B Present your conversation to another pair. Observe their conversation.

AT WORK ▶ **Introducing others**

🔊 1-24 **A** Listen and read the conversations. What are the correct names in each conversation?

1. **A:** This is Larry.

   B: Barry?

   A: No, Larry.

   B: Oh, sorry. Hello, Larry.

2. **A:** This is Simone.

   B: Can you repeat that, please?

   A: Simone.

   B: Nice to meet you, Simone.

B Work with two partners. Take turns introducing each other. Practice checking for correct information.

▶▶ **TEST YOURSELF**

Walk around the classroom. Greet and introduce yourself to your classmates. Check the pronunciation of their names.

1 Build reading strategies

A Look at the pictures. Read the sentences. How do you study English? Check (✓) the boxes.

I'm a student.

☐ Read English. ☐ Go to school. ☐ Speak English. ☐ Ask for help.

B Preview the poster below.

1. What is the title?
2. What is the poster about?

READER'S NOTE

Think about the **title** before you read.

Set a Goal! Learn more English!

★ Study every day.

★ Speak English at home.

★ Go to school.

★ Listen to English on the radio.

★ Ask your classmates and teacher for help.

C Read the poster silently.

D Listen and read the poster again. How many of these things do you do?
1-25

E Read the questions. Fill in the bubble next to the correct answer.

1. Ask your _____ for help.
   - (a) teacher
   - (b) pencil
   - (c) radio

2. _____ to English on the radio.
   - (a) Speak
   - (b) Listen
   - (c) Read

3. Go to _____ .
   - (a) school
   - (b) English
   - (c) students

4. _____ English every day.
   - (a) Read
   - (b) Write
   - (c) a and b

2 Name your goals

A Why do you study English? Check (✓) the pictures.

☐ school and my children

☐ work

☐ conversation and fun

☐ United States citizenship

☐ my health

☐ shopping

☐ job training

☐ college degree

B Work with your classmates. Count the checks (✓) for each picture. What are some important goals for you and your classmates?

⏻ BRING IT TO LIFE

Find a way to practice English on your phone or on a computer. Share it with your classmates.

TEAMWORK & LANGUAGE REVIEW

A Work with a team. Look at the picture. Write words you know in the chart.

Things	Actions (verbs)	Other
books	listen	teacher

B Point to things and people in the picture. Take turns asking and answering questions in your group.

A: *Who is she?*

B: *She's…*

A: *What is it?*

B: *It's…*

A: *Who are they?*

B: *They're…*

A: *What are they?*

B: *They're…*

C Look up three words you don't know in a dictionary. Add them to the chart.

D Work with your class. Write sentences about the picture.

Nancy and Sasi are students. They're not teachers.

E Interview three classmates who are not in your group. Write their answers in the chart.

First name	Last name

NEED HELP?

What is your first name?

What is your last name?

Can you repeat that, please?

Please spell that.

Thank you. See you later!

ACADEMIC

F Work with your group. Put the names in one list. Use alphabetical order by last name.

Jai Nabil

Tan Nyugen

Dora Sanchez

PROBLEM SOLVING

A Listen and read. Look at the picture. What is the problem?

1-26

Today is the first day of class at Pass Street Adult School. The teacher is Nora Jackson. Jose Ortiz is a student.

B Work with your classmates. Answer the question: What can Jose say to Nora?

a. Good morning.

b. Good evening. I'm Jose Ortiz.

c. See you later, Nora.

d. Other: _____

UNIT
2 Can You Help Me?

A LOOK AT
- Days, dates, and time
- Questions with *be*
- Asking for help

LESSON 1 VOCABULARY

1 Learn about telling time

A Show what you know. Circle the words you use.

1. eight o'clock
2. nine fifteen a.m.
3. noon
4. eight thirty p.m.
5. nine forty-five p.m.
6. midnight

1 Good morning.

8:00 a.m.

2

9:15 a.m.

3

12:00 p.m.

4 Good evening.

8:30 p.m.

5

9:45 p.m.

6 Good night.

12:00 a.m.

B Listen and look at the pictures. When is lunch?
1-27

C Listen and repeat the words from 1A.
1-28

D Match the sentences with the times.

___e___ 1. It's eight o'clock in the morning.
_____ 2. It's midnight.
_____ 3. It's eight thirty in the evening.
_____ 4. It's nine forty-five in the evening.
_____ 5. It's noon.

a. 8:30 p.m.
b. 9:45 p.m.
c. 12:00 a.m.
d. 12:00 p.m.
e. 8:00 a.m.

NEED HELP?

8:00 a.m. *or*
8:00 in the morning

12:00 p.m. *or* noon

8:30 p.m. *or*
8:30 in the evening

12:00 a.m. *or* midnight

E Work with a partner. Ask and answer questions about the pictures in 1A.

A: What time is it?

B: It's eight o'clock in the morning.

2 Talk about a calendar

🔊 1-29 **A** Listen. Repeat the months.

1. January	3. March	5. May	7. July	9. September	11. November
2. February	4. April	6. June	8. August	10. October	12. December

B Work in a team. Match the words with the numbers on the calendar.

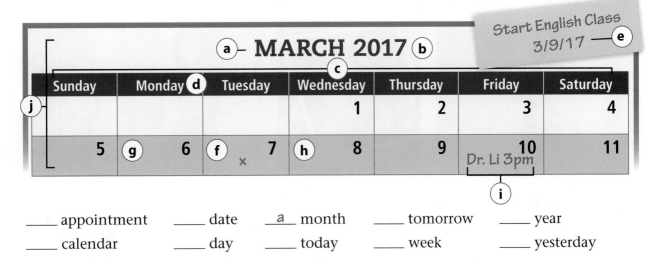

____ appointment	____ date	_a_ month
____ calendar	____ day	____ today

____ tomorrow	____ year
____ week	____ yesterday

🔊 1-30 **C** Listen and check your answers. Then practice the words with a partner.

D Complete the chart. Use the words in the box.

Year	~~Times~~	Days	Months

Times			
5:00	Monday	January	1870
7:30	Wednesday	March	1999
12:10	Friday	September	2017

E Talk to a partner. Ask and answer the questions.

1. What time is it?
2. What are the days of the week?
3. What's your favorite day of the week? Why?
4. What's your favorite month of the year? Why?

▶▶ **TEST YOURSELF**

Use your notebook. Copy this chart.
Put 4 words from the lesson in
each column.

Times of day	Days	Months

1 Prepare to write

A Look at the pictures. Who are the people?

B Look at the pictures again. Listen to the story.

1-31

My favorite color is purple.

C Listen again and read the story.

1-31

> My Story
>
> by Irma Chavez
>
> My name is Irma Chavez. I live in California. I'm from Mexico.
> My date of birth is January 7th, 1991. My favorite color
> is purple. I'm a student at City Community College.

D Check your understanding. Circle the correct words.

1. Irma is a (student / teacher).
2. She is from (California / Mexico).
3. She lives in (California / Mexico).
4. Irma's favorite color is (purple / January).

E Listen to the students. Complete their stories.

1-32

1. His _____ is James.
2. He _____ from China.
3. His favorite color is _____ .

4. Her name is _____ .
5. She's _____ Vietnam.
6. _____ lives in Florida.
7. Her favorite color is _____ .

NEED HELP?

Colors

red		orange	
blue		purple	
yellow		pink	
green		brown	
gray		tan	
black		white	

2 Plan

A Listen and repeat.

1-33

A: What's your name?

B: My name is Tara. What's your name?

A: Where are you from?

B: I'm from India.

A: Where do you live now?

B: I live in Texas.

A: What's your birthdate?

B: My birthdate is June 12, 1994.

B Work with a partner. Practice the conversation. Use your own information.

3 Write

A Write your story. Complete the sentences.

My Story

by _____

My name is _____ . I'm from

_____ . My date of birth is

_____ . I live in _____ .

My favorite color is _____ .

> **WRITER'S NOTE**
> April 25, 1994
> Use a comma between the day and the year.

B Share your story. Read your story to a partner.

▶▶ TEST YOURSELF

Complete the following sentences. Share your responses with your teacher.

1. After this writing lesson, I can…

2. I need more help with…

1 Explore *yes/no* questions and answers with *be*: meaning and form

A Look at the pictures. Read the questions and answers. Then answer the question: *How do you feel*?

A: Is Trang happy?
B: Yes, he is.

A: Is Maria worried?
B: Yes, she is.

A: Is the dog hungry?
B: Yes, it is.

A: Are Raj and Padma worried?
B: No, they aren't. They're proud.

A: Is Jake happy?
B: No, he isn't. He's angry.

A: Is Paul angry?
B: No, he isn't. He's tired.

B Work with the grammar. Look at 1A. What is the first word in each question? Circle it.

C Study the form. Read the charts.

Yes/no questions with *be*								
Questions				**Answers**				
Are	you				I am.			I'm not.
Is	he she it	hungry? tired? happy?		Yes,	he is. she is. it is.		No,	he isn't. she isn't. it isn't.
Are	you they				we are. they are.			we aren't. they aren't.

D Work with a partner. Look at the charts in 1C. Ask and answer questions.

2 Practice: ask and answer questions with *be*

A Listen to the questions about the picture. Circle *a* or *b*.
1-34

1. a. Yes, she is. b. No, she isn't.
2. a. Yes, he is. b. No, he isn't.
3. a. Yes, they are. b. No, they aren't.
4. a. Yes, it is. b. Yes, they are.
5. a. Yes, it is. b. No, it isn't.
6. a. Yes, it is. b. No, it isn't.

B Look at the picture in 2A. Complete the questions and answers.

1. **A:** _____ Nancy angry?
   B: No, she _____ .
2. **A:** Are _____ at work?
   B: Yes, they _____ .
3. **A:** Is _____ morning?
   B: No, it isn't. _____ evening.
4. **A:** _____ today Monday?
   B: _____ , it is.
5. **A:** Is _____ November?
   B: No, _____ _____ . _____ April.
6. **A:** _____ the chairs green?
   B: No, _____ _____ . They're _____ .

C Talk to a partner. Ask and answer questions. Use the adjectives in the box.

open	closed	tired	hungry	black	white

A: *Is the book open?*   **A:** *Are the computers white?*
B: *Yes, it is.*   **B:** *No, they aren't. They're black.*

GRAMMAR NOTE

Adjectives
green
happy
worried
good
fine
new

3 Practice questions with *or*

1-35

A Study the form. Listen to the questions and answers. Underline the words before and after *or*. Which ones are adjectives?

Or questions	
A: Are you happy or angry? **B:** I'm happy.	**A:** Are they pens or pencils? **B:** They're pencils.
A: Is she a teacher or a student? **B:** She's a student.	**A:** Are the classes in the morning or the evening? **B:** They're in the evening.

B Work with the grammar. Match the questions with the answers.

___d___ 1. Is Todd happy or angry?   a. They're yellow.

_____ 2. Are the pencils green or yellow?   b. She's a student.

_____ 3. Is the woman a student or a teacher?   c. It's blue.

_____ 4. Are the students at home or at school?   d. He's angry.

_____ 5. Is your pen black or blue?   e. They're at school.

4 Ask and answer *yes/no* questions and *or* questions

A Work with a group to write questions about people and things in your classroom. Use *or*.

1. Is the board __black__ or __white__ ?

2. Is _____ a student or a teacher?

3. Are you _____ or _____ ?

4. Is _____ ?

5. Are _____ ?

6. _____ ?

Is it morning or evening?

It's morning!

B Talk to students from other teams. Ask your questions.

▶▶ TEST YOURSELF

Close your book. Write two *yes/no* questions and one question with *or*. Ask and answer the questions with a partner.

1 Listen to learn: marital status

A Listen and look at the pictures. Read the sentences. Then answer the questions below.

1-36

① I'm single.

Ms. Lopez is a single woman. She isn't married.

1. Are you single? _____

② I'm single.

Mr. Madaki is a single man. He isn't married.

2. Are you married? _____

③ We're married.

Mr. and Mrs. Okada are a married couple. They aren't single.

2 Practice your pronunciation

A Listen and repeat the names. Pay attention to the pronunciation of *Miss*, *Mrs.*, *Mr.*, and *Ms.*

1-37

Miss Aroyan	Mrs. Lee	Mr. Jones	Ms. Sanchez
Miss Martin	Mrs. Ball	Mr. Singh	Ms. Waffa

B Listen and write the correct title for each name. Use *Miss*, *Ms.*, *Mrs.*, or *Mr.*

1-38

1. __Mrs.__ Tyson
2. _____ Song
3. _____ Miller
4. _____ Farmer
5. _____ Silver
6. _____ Gold

C Work with a partner. Say the names in 2B.

D Discuss titles. Talk about the questions with your class.

1. When do you use first names?
2. When do you use *Mr./Ms./Mrs.* + last name?

NEED HELP?

Mrs. = a married woman

Miss = a single woman

Ms. = a married or single woman

Mr. = a married or single man

3 Practice personal information questions

🔊 **A** Listen and read. Where is Mrs. Wong?

1-39

🔊 **B** Look at 3A. Listen to the questions. Write the answers.

1-40

1. _____ 2. _____ 3. _____

C Think about the grammar.

1. Underline the question with *or* and the question with *Where are*.

2. Which question is about a place?

3. Which question asks for a choice?

D Talk to a partner about 3A. Ask and answer the questions in the chart.

Information questions	*Yes/no* questions	*Or* questions
What's the man's name?	Is Jon at work?	Is Mrs. Wong from China or Korea?
Where is Mrs. Wong?	Is Mrs. Wong from Peru?	Is the form blue or yellow?

4 Make conversation: giving personal information

A Work with a partner. Make a conversation. Use your own ideas.

A: _____ ?

B: No, I'm not.

A: _____ with this form?

B: Sure. Write your _____ here. Are you _____ or single?

A: I'm _____ .

B: OK. Fill in the _____ bubble.

And where are you from, _____ ?

A: I'm from _____ .

B: Write _____ next to "place of birth."

B Present your conversation to another pair. Observe their conversation.

AT WORK ▸ Asking for help

A Listen and read the conversations. How do they ask for help?

1-41

1. **A:** Are you busy?

   B: No, I'm not.

   A: Could you help me with this form?

   B: Sure.

2. **A:** Excuse me. I need some help.

   B: I'm a little busy now. Come back at 1:00.

   A: OK. No problem.

B Work with a partner. Practice the conversations in A.

C Think about it. Who can you ask for help at work? At school?

▸▸ TEST YOURSELF

Find a new partner. Have the conversation in A. Student A: Look in the book.
Student B: Close your book. Take turns.

1 **Build reading strategies**

A Look at the pictures. Read the words. How many countries are in each picture?

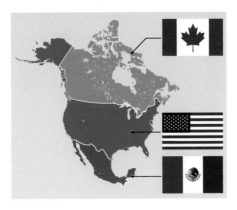

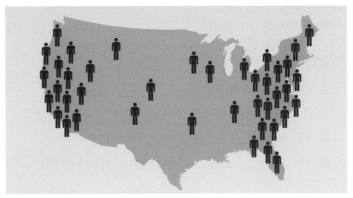

countries   population

B Talk to your classmates. Find your country on a map. What countries are you and your classmates from?

C Preview the article. Find the footnote. What is the word for 1,000,000?

READER'S NOTE

D Read the article.

People in the United States: Where are they from?

The population of the United States is about 319 million[1] people. Today, 42 million people in the U.S. are from other countries. Where are they from?

• 22 million are from Latin America.
• 13 million are from Asia.
• 7 million are from Europe, Africa, and Australia.

[1]million = 1,000,000

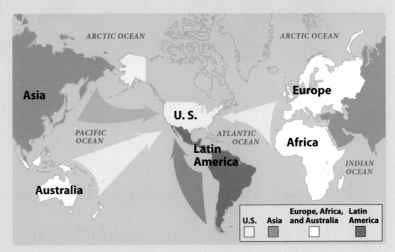

Source: *U.S. Census Bureau*

 E Listen and read the article in 1D again.

1-42

F Mark the sentences *T* (true) or *F* (false).

_____ 1. The population of the United States is 319 million.

_____ 2. Seven million people are from Asia.

_____ 3. 22 million people in the United States are from Latin America.

_____ 4. Asia is in Latin America.

_____ 5. The information in the article is from the Migration Policy Institute.

2 Read more about the U.S. population

A Look at the graph. What countries are people in the United States from?

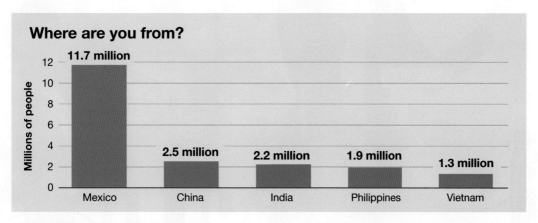

Source: *U.S. Census Bureau*

B Work with your classmates. Make a graph about your class.

Where are you and your classmates from?

Numbers of classmates

C Write sentences about your graph.

Seven students are from South Korea.

⏻ BRING IT TO LIFE

Complete this question with the name of a country. Type the question into a search engine on a computer or on your phone. Write the answer. Tell your classmates.

How many people in the U.S. are from _____? _____

TEAMWORK & LANGUAGE REVIEW

A Work with a team. Look at the picture. Match the questions with the answers.

<u>d</u> 1. What day is it?

_____ 2. Is it morning or evening?

_____ 3. Are they happy?

_____ 4. What's Mrs. Taylor's favorite color?

_____ 5. Is it 8 p.m.?

a. It's morning.

b. No, it isn't.

c. No, they aren't.

d. It's Monday.

e. It's blue.

B Work with a team. Write 4-5 new questions about the picture.

Who…?   Is…?   Are…?   What…?

C Talk to people from other teams. Ask your questions.

D Work with your class. Write sentences about the picture.

Today is Monday.

E Interview three classmates from other teams. Write their answers in the chart.

1. What's your name?

2. Where are you from?

3. Are you married or single?

4. What's your favorite color?

Classmate's name	Place of birth	Married or single	Favorite color

F Work with your team. Share your data. Are most of your classmates married or single? What colors do most people like?

PROBLEM SOLVING

A Look at the picture. What is the problem?

B Work with your classmates. Answer the question. What can Bella do? More than one answer is possible.

a. Give the form to the teacher.

b. Read the form to the teacher.

c. Ask for a new form.

d. Other: _____

People in Our Lives

LESSON **1** VOCABULARY

1 Learn about family members

A Show what you know. Circle the words you use.

1. husband	3. father	5. mother	7. parents	9. grandmother
2. wife	4. son	6. daughter	8. children*	10. grandfather

one child / two children

The
Martinez
Family

Carlos and Anita are married!
6/22/07

Carlos and and baby Eric
11/15/10

Anita and baby Robin
4/20/14

Helen, Ramiro, Carlos, Anita, Eric, and Robin
6/30/17

B Listen and look at the pictures. What is the boy's name? What is the girl's name?
1-43

C Listen and repeat the words from 1A.
1-44

D Write the vocabulary. Look at the pictures. Complete the sentences.

1. Anita is a ___wife___ and ___mother___ .
2. Eric is a _____ .
3. Eric and Robin are _____ .
4. Carlos is a _____ and _____ .
5. Carlos and Anita are _____ .
6. Robin is a _____ .
7. Helen is a _____ and a _____ .
8. Ramiro is a _____ and a _____ .

2 Talk about a family

A Work in a team. Match the words with the pictures.

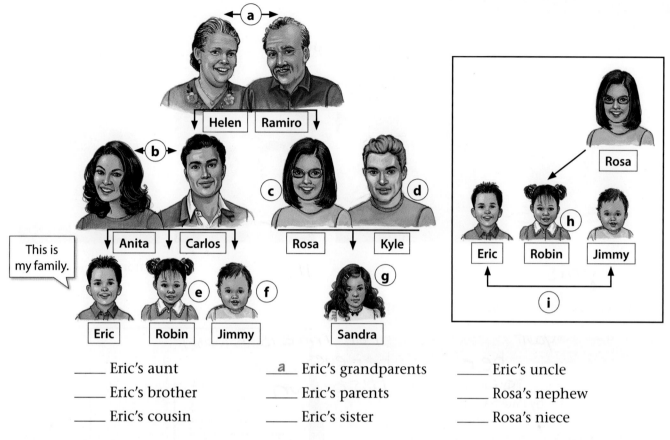

This is my family.

____ Eric's aunt   _a_ Eric's grandparents   ____ Eric's uncle

____ Eric's brother   ____ Eric's parents   ____ Rosa's nephew

____ Eric's cousin   ____ Eric's sister   ____ Rosa's niece

B Listen and check your answers. Then practice the words with a partner.

1-45

C Think about it. These words describe family by marriage. Look at the picture in 2A. Then answer the questions.

mother-in-law	father-in-law	sister-in-law
brother-in-law	son-in-law	daughter-in-law

1. Who is Anita's mother-in-law? _____

2. Who is Anita's sister-in-law? _____

3. Who is Anita's brother-in-law? _____

4. Who is Ramiro and Helen's son-in-law? _____

D Listen to Anita and check your answers. Then ask and answer the questions with a partner.

1-46

▶▶ **TEST YOURSELF**

Use your notebook. Copy this chart. Put words from the lesson in the chart. Check your spelling.

Man	Woman	Both

1 Prepare to write

A Talk about the pictures below. Who are the people?

B Look at the pictures. Listen to the paragraph.
1-47

Sam   Karina   Simon

C Listen again and read the paragraph.
1-47

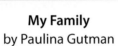

My Family
by Paulina Gutman

My name is Paulina Gutman. Let me tell you about my family. Sam is my son. He is the tall boy with blond hair. Karina is my daughter. She is the girl with brown hair and big blue eyes. My husband is the short man with beautiful gray hair. His name is Simon. They are all very special to me.

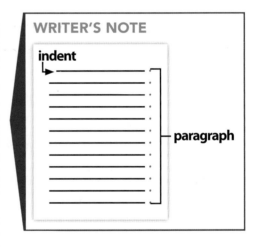

WRITER'S NOTE

indent

paragraph

D Check your understanding. Match the numbers with the letters.

___e___ 1. Paulina
_____ 2. Karina
_____ 3. Simon
_____ 4. Sam
_____ 5. Sam and Karina

a. brown hair and blue eyes
b. short with gray hair
c. tall with blond hair
d. children
e. blond hair and blue eyes

🔊 **E Listen to Paulina. Who is the man in the picture?**
1-48

🔊 **F Listen again. Answer the questions.**
1-48

1. What's his name? ____Albert____ .

2. Is he tall or short? _____ .

3. What color are his eyes? _____ .

4. What color is his hair? _____ .

2 Plan

A Get ready to write. Think about a family member or friend. Complete the information.

Name: _____   Eye color: _____

Hair color: _____   Tall or short? _____

NEED HELP?
Colors for eyes
■ black   ■ brown
■ blue   ■ green
Colors for hair
■ black   ■ brown
▨ blond   ▨ gray
■ red   □ white

3 Write

A Write a paragraph about your family member or friend.

My _____

My name is _____ . Let me tell you about my
_____ . His/Her* name is _____ . His/Her hair
is _____ . His/Her eyes are _____ . He/She is
very special to me.

*Circle *His* for a man or *Her* for a woman.

B Share your description. Read your paragraph to a partner. Then copy it into your notebook.

▶▶**TEST YOURSELF**

Complete the following sentences. Share your responses with your teacher.

1. After this writing lesson, I can…
2. I need more help with…

1 Explore possessive adjectives and nouns: meaning and form

A Listen and read Joe's story. What color are Charlie's eyes?

1-49

My name is Joe. This is my daughter. Her name is Grace. This is my grandson. He is a great kid. His name is Charlie. Charlie's eyes are brown. His hair is blond. My eyes are green, but brown eyes are my favorite.

B Analyze the sentences in 1A. Is *her* for a man or a woman? Is *his* for a man or a woman? What does *Charlie's eyes* mean?

C Study the form. Read the charts.

Possessive Adjectives		
Pronouns	**Possessive adjectives**	**Examples**
I	my	My eyes are green.
you	your	Your eyes are blue.
he	his	His eyes are brown.
she	her	Her eyes are blue.
it	its	Its eyes are yellow.
we	our	Our eyes are blue.
you	your	Your eyes are brown.
they	their	Their eyes are green.

D Look at the picture in 1A. Circle the correct words.

1. (Her / Their) name is Grace.

2. (His / Her) name is Charlie. His hair (is / are) blond.

3. (Their / Your) names (is / are) Grace and Charlie.

4. Grace is a mother. Charlie is (his / her) son.

2 Practice: possessives

A Listen to the statements about the picture. Circle *True* or *False*.

1-50

1. True False	3. True False	5. True False	
2. True False	4. True False	6. True False	

B Look at the picture in 2A. Read the grammar note. Circle the correct words.

1. This is a picture of Mena and (his / her) family.
2. Mark is Mena's father. (My / His) eyes are green.
3. Sachi is (Deyva's / Mena's) mother.
4. Tomas is (her / your) son.
5. (They're / Their) at home.
6. (Their / Its) house is green.

> **GRAMMAR NOTE**
>
> Use **'s** after a name for the possessive.
> Mena**'s** eyes = her eyes
> Mark**'s** wife = his wife
> The family**'s** house = their house

C Talk to a partner. Follow the directions.

Student A: Make true and false statements about the picture in 2A.

Student B: Say *That's true.* or *That's false.*

A: *Her name is Mena. Her eyes are brown.*   A: *His name is Mark. His hair is red.*

B: *That's true. Her eyes are brown.*   B: *That's false. His hair is gray.*

3 Practice information questions with possessives

A Study the form. Listen and repeat the questions and answers. Underline *It* and *They* in the answers. What do they refer to?

1-51

Information questions and answers with possessives	
A: What color is Mena's hair? **B:** Her hair is brown. (It's brown.)	**A:** What color is Mark's hair? **B:** His hair is gray. (It's gray.) *hair*
A: What color are Mena's eyes? **B:** Her eyes are green. (They're green.)	**A:** What color are Mark's eyes? **B:** His eyes are green. (They're green.)

B Work with the grammar. Complete the answers.

1. **A:** Who is Mena's grandmother?

   B: _Her_ name is Deyva.

2. **A:** Who is Sachi's husband?

   B: _his_ name is Mark.

   _su_

3. **A:** What is their daughter's name?

   B: _her_ name is Mena.

4. **A:** What color is _their_ house?

   B: _It is_ green.

C Write about your teacher. Complete the questions. Write the answers.

1. What's _your_ teacher's name? _her name is Elizabet_
2. What color are _her_ eyes? _her eyes by_
3. What color _is_ her hair? _It's brown_

4 Ask and answer questions about your classmates

A Read the questions in the chart. Write your answers.

Questions	My answers	My partner's answers
1. What's your name?		
2. What color are your eyes?		
3. What color is your hair?		

B Talk to a partner. Ask and answer the questions. Write your partner's answers in the chart.

C Talk about the answers in the chart with your class.

His name is Asim. Asim's eyes are green. His hair is black.

▶▶ TEST YOURSELF

Close your book. Write four sentences. Describe your classmates and your teacher.

My teacher's hair is brown.

1 Listen to learn: ordinal numbers

A Look at the calendar. Which words are new to you?

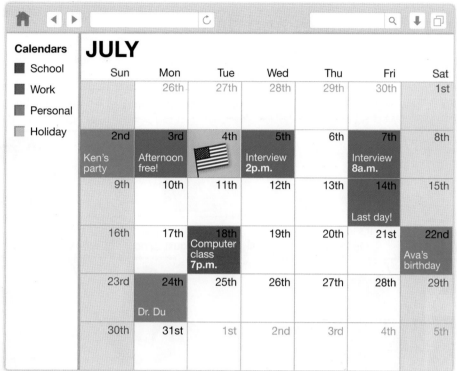

NEED HELP?

Months of the year

January
February
March
April
May
June
July
August
September
October
November
December

Dates

1st = first
2nd = second
3rd = third
4th = fourth
5th = fifth
20th = twentieth
21st = twenty-first

🔊 **B** Listen and look at the calendar. Why is July 4th yellow?
1-52　　What is on July 14th?

2 Practice your pronunciation

🔊 **A** Listen and repeat the numbers in the chart. Pay attention to the end of each word.
1-53

-st	-nd	-rd	-th
fir**st**	seco**nd**	thi**rd**	four**th**
twenty-fir**st**	twenty-seco**nd**	twenty-thi**rd**	twenty-four**th**

🔊 **B** Listen. Circle *a* or *b*.
1-54

1. a. 1st
   (b.) 3rd

2. a. 23rd
   (b.) 26th

3. (a.) 7th
   b. 2nd

4. a. 4th
   b. 14th

5. a. 1st
   b. 21st

6. a. 3rd
   (b.) 23rd

C Listen and write the dates you hear.

1. May 12th
2. Jun 9th
3. April 15th
4. Sept 25th
5. Jan 2 nd
6. March 3rd
7. October 8th
8. Nov 1st

D Work with a partner. Say the dates in 2C. Take turns.

3 Practice talking about times and dates

A Listen and read the conversation. When is Ashley's party?

a
Hi, Koji. This is Ashley.
Hi, Ashley. What's up?

b
Is your sister at home?
No, she's not. She's usually at home in the evening.

c
OK. Is her party on August 22nd?
No, it's in September. On the 2nd.

d
Oh good! My party is on August 22nd.
I know. At 5:00. Don't worry. It's on our calendar!

B Listen and circle the answers to the questions.

1. a. in the morning
   b. in the evening

2. a. on August 22nd
   b. on September 2nd

3. a. at 4:00
   b. at 5:00

C Think about the grammar. Look at the conversation and answer the question.

1. Say the words for days, months, dates, and times.

2. Do we use *in* or *on* with dates? With months?

D Work with a partner. Use the chart to answer the questions. Use your own information.

Time Prepositions	
The interview is **at** 8:00. The class is from 9:00 **to** 11:00. The appointment is **on** Monday. Her birthday is **in** April.	morning. The class is **in** the afternoon. evening.

1. What time is your English class?

2. What day is your next English class?

3. What's the date of your last English class?

4. Are you usually at home in the morning? In the evening?

5. What month is your birthday?

4 Make conversation: talking about dates

A Work with a partner. Make a new conversation.

A: Hi. This is _____ .

B: Hi, _____ . What's up?

A: Is your _____ at home?

B: No, he/she isn't. He's/she's usually home in the _____ .

A: Is his/her _____ on _____ ?

B: Yes. It's on _____ at _____ .

NEED HELP?

Things on a calendar
party
appointment
interview
class
first day of work

B Present your conversation to another pair. Observe their conversation.

AT WORK ▶ Using voicemail

A Listen to the outgoing messages and look at the pictures. Why isn't Paul at work?

1-58

1. Hi. This is Joan. I'm away from my desk. Please leave a message.

2. Hi. This is Don. I'm out of the office. Please leave a message.

3. Hi. This is Paul. The shop is closed from Thursday, November 23rd to Sunday, November 26th. Please call back next week!

B Work with a partner. Practice saying the outgoing messages in A. Make an outgoing message for your home or job.

Hi. This is _____ . I'm _____ . Please _____ .

▶▶TEST YOURSELF

Work with a partner. Sit back to back. Take turns with each role.

Student A: Say the outgoing message on your voicemail.
Student B: Leave a message. Ask about an appointment or a party.

1 Build reading strategies

A Look at the pictures. Read the words. Count the adults in each picture.

1

2

3

4

adult children   young children   large family   small family

B Work with your classmates. Answer the questions. More than one answer is possible.

1. How many children are in a large family?

2. How many children are in a small family?

C Preview the article. Look at the pie chart. What percentage of families have no children?

D Read the article.

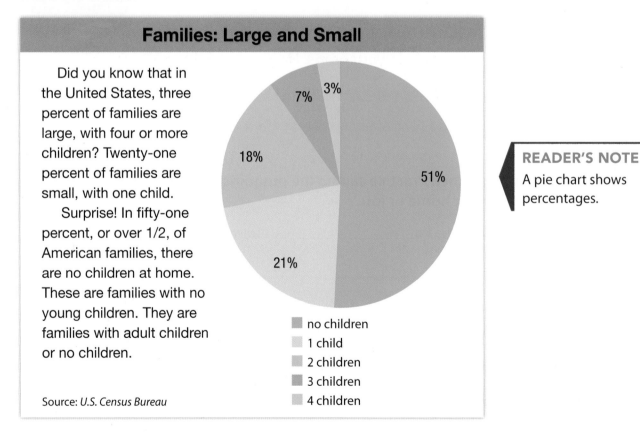

Families: Large and Small

Did you know that in the United States, three percent of families are large, with four or more children? Twenty-one percent of families are small, with one child.

Surprise! In fifty-one percent, or over 1/2, of American families, there are no children at home. These are families with no young children. They are families with adult children or no children.

Source: *U.S. Census Bureau*

7% 3%
18%
51%
21%

READER'S NOTE
A pie chart shows percentages.

■ no children
■ 1 child
■ 2 children
■ 3 children
■ 4 children

E Listen and read the article in 1D again. Where is your family on the pie chart?
1-59

F **Read the questions. Fill in the bubble next to the correct answer.**

1. Three percent of families in the United States have _____ .
   - (a) 1 child
   - (b) 3 children
   - (c) 4+ children

2. Twenty-one percent of families in the United States _____ .
   - (a) are small
   - (b) are large
   - (c) have many young children

3. Over one half of American families have _____ .
   - (a) one or two children at home
   - (b) three or more children at home
   - (c) no children at home

4. The writer says "surprise!" because many families _____ .
   - (a) have four or more children
   - (b) have two or more children
   - (c) have no children at home

G **Match the letters in the chart with the sentences. Look at the article in 1D for help.**

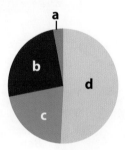

_____ 1. families with one child

_____ 2. families with two or three children

_____ 3. families with four or more children

_____ 4. families with no children at home

2 Make a chart with your classmates

A **Think about the people in your home. How many children are there?**

B **Work with your classmates. Complete the chart.**

Number of children at home				
	1 child	2–3 children	4 or more children	no children
Number of classmates with:				

C **Talk about the answer with your class.**

Five people have one child.

D **Work with your classmates. Talk about the questions.**

1. Is your class chart different from the chart in 1D?

2. Does the information in the chart surprise you?

3. What is interesting about your class chart?

 BRING IT TO LIFE

Find pictures of families on the Internet. Bring the pictures to class. Talk about the pictures with your classmates.

A Work with a team. Look at the picture. Match the questions with the answers.

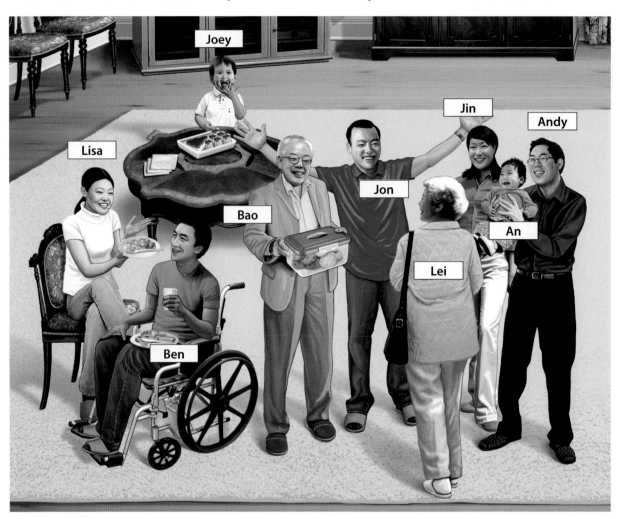

___c__ 1. What color is Jon's hair?

_____ 2. Is it 3 a.m.?

_____ 3. What color are Ben's eyes?

_____ 4. Who is Jin?

_____ 5. Where are they?

a. They're brown.

b. No, it isn't.

c. It's black.

d. They're at a party.

e. She's Andy's wife.

B Work with a team. Write 5-6 new questions about the picture.

Who...?   What...?   Is...?   Are...?

C Talk to people from other teams. Ask your questions.

D Work with your class. Write a paragraph about Ben.

Today is February 4th. Ben is...

E Interview three classmates from other teams. Write their answers in the chart.

1. What's your favorite month?

2. What's your favorite day of the week?

3. What's your favorite date of the year?

Classmate's name	Favorite day	Favorite month	Favorite date

F Work with your team. Share your data. What do most of your classmates like?

G Work with your class. Why do people like a day, month, or date? Discuss the reasons.

PROBLEM SOLVING

1-60

A Listen and read about Miguel. What is the problem?

Today is Miguel's first day of work. This is his new employee ID card. Miguel is not happy with the card. There's a problem.

Miguel Ramirez

123 First Street

Big City, CA

91100

Eyes: brown

Hair: blond

Date of birth: 11/09/94

Miguel Ramirez

B Work with your classmates. Answer the question. What can Miguel do? More than one answer is possible.

a. Ask a co-worker.

b. Tell the boss.

c. Say nothing about it.

d. Other: _____

UNIT

4 At Home

A LOOK AT
- Home life
- Present continuous
- Stating problems

LESSON **1** VOCABULARY

1 Learn about places and things in the home

A Show what you know. Circle the words you use.

1. garage
2. living room
3. bathroom
4. bedroom
5. dining area
6. kitchen
7. roof
8. door
9. floor
10. wall

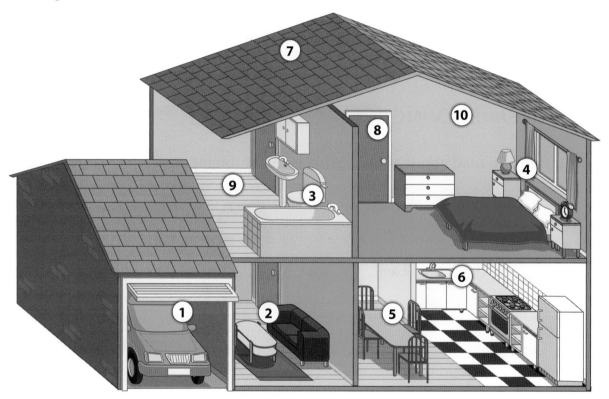

1-61
B Listen and look at the picture. Do they like the house?

1-62
C Listen and repeat the words from 1A.

D Write the vocabulary. Look at the picture. Complete the sentences.

1. The living room _____wall_____ is green.
2. The kitchen _____ is black and white.
3. The _____ is yellow.
4. The _____ is gray.
5. The _____ walls are pink.
6. The _____ floor is blue.

E Ask and answer these questions with your partner.

A: What's your favorite room at home?

B: My favorite room is _____ .

2 Talk about things in the home

A Work in a team. Match the words with the pictures.

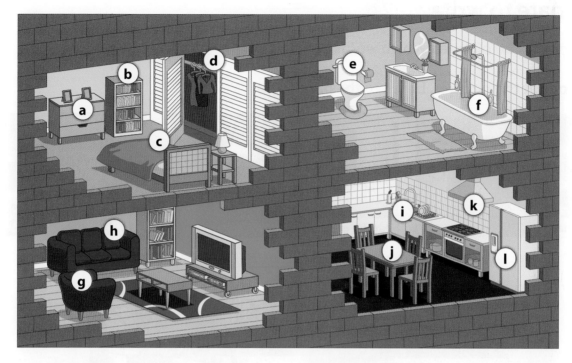

_____ bathtub	_____ chair	_____ refrigerator	_____ stove
_____ bed	_____ closet	_____ sink	_____ table
_____ bookcase	_____ dresser	_____ sofa	_____ toilet

B Listen and check your answers.

1-63

C Say and spell the words with a partner.

A: Can you spell _____ ?

B: Sure. It's __ __ __ __ __ __ __ __ .

D Talk to a partner. Ask and answer questions about the home in 1A on page 46.

A: Where's the toilet?   A: Is the table in the kitchen?   A: Is the bed in the bedroom?

B: It's in the bathroom.   B: No, it isn't.   B: Yes, it is.

E Think about it. Ask and answer the questions with your classmates.

1. What places have sinks? Sofas? Bookcases?

2. What other places have dining areas? Garages? Closets?

▶▶ TEST YOURSELF

Use your notebook. Copy this chart. Put words from the lesson in the chart. Which words go in more than one place?

Kitchen	Living room	Bedroom

1 Prepare to write

A Look at the pictures. Which words do you know?

🔊
1-64 **B** Look at the pictures. Listen to the paragraph.

roommates

cut the grass

watch TV

play video games

cook

🔊
1-64 **C** Listen again and read the paragraph.

Sundays at Our Place
by Sam Lopez

My roommates and I go to City Lake College. We are at home today. Robert is in the yard. He's cutting the grass. Simon is watching TV in the living room. Julio and Luis are in the bedroom. They're playing a video game. And me? I'm cooking dinner and listening to music with my friend, Alma. Sundays are great at our place.

WRITER'S NOTE
The author names the people in his story. Names help the reader "see" the people in the story.

D Check your understanding. Mark the sentences *T* (true) or *F* (false).

___T___ 1. Robert is in the yard.

_____ 2. Simon is listening to music.

_____ 3. Julio and Luis are in the bedroom.

_____ 4. Sam and Alma are in the kitchen.

_____ 5. Alma is cooking.

_____ 6. Sam is playing a video game.

E Listen and complete the sentences.

1-65

1. Joe is _____ *in the living room* _____ .

2. Mia is _____ .

3. Sam and Lisa are _____ .

4. Tasha _____ .

5. It's _____ .

F Compare sentences with your partner. Listen again and check your work.

1-65

2 Plan

A Draw yourself and your family, roommates, or friends at home.

Who is he?

Where is he?

B Talk about your picture with your classmates.

Tell me about him.

3 Write

A Write a paragraph about your picture.

> **A Day in My Home**
> by _____
>
> In this picture, my _____ and
> I are at home. I am in the _____ .
> _____ is in the _____ . It's a
> _____ day at my home.

NEED HELP?

It's a _____ day.

- good
- great
- special
- nice
- quiet

B Share your story. Read your paragraph to a partner.

▶▶ **TEST YOURSELF**

Complete the following sentences. Share your responses with your teacher.

1. After this writing lesson, I can…
2. I need more help with…

1 Explore the present continuous: meaning and form

A **Look at the pictures. Read the sentences. Who is at home? Who is at work?**

Marta **is cleaning** the living room. She**'s not cleaning** the bathroom.

Mario **is washing** the windows. He**'s not washing** the dishes.

Pam and Sue **are eating** lunch. They**'re not eating** breakfast.

I**'m writing**. I**'m not** reading.

John and I **are sweeping**. We**'re not mopping**.

The cat **is sleeping**. It**'s not playing**.

B **Analyze the sentences in 1A. What do you notice? Are all the sentences true? How do you know?**

C **Study the form. Read the charts.**

The Present Continuous						
Statements						
I	am	eating. writing. sleeping.	You		eating. writing. sleeping.
You	are		We	are	
He She It	is		They		

Negative statements						
I	am not	eating. writing. sleeping.	You		eating. writing. sleeping.
You	are not		We	are not	
He She It	is not		They		

GRAMMAR NOTE

he's not = he isn't
she's not = she isn't
you're not = you aren't
we're not = we aren't
they're not = they aren't

D **Work with a partner. Look at the charts in 1C. How many sentences can you make?**

2 Practice: present continuous statements

A Listen to the statements about the picture. Circle _True_ or _False_.

1-66

1. True (False)   3. True   False   5. (True)   False
2. (True)   False   4. True   False   6. True   (False)

B Look at the picture in 2A. Complete the sentences.

1. Alma _'s____ listening to music. She' _s____ _not__ eating.
2. Jen _____ sweeping the floor. She'_____ _____
   mopping the floor.
3. Van and Jen _____ working. They'_____ _____ studying.
4. Rob _____ sleeping. _____ _____
   reading.
5. Franco is _____ in a notebook. _____
   _____ eating lunch.

> **SPELLING NOTE**
>
> write → writing (e)
> smile → smiling (e)
>
> cut → cutting
> mop → mopping
> sit → sitting

C Talk to a partner. Follow the directions.

Student A: Make true and false statements about the picture in 2A.

Student B: Say: _That's true._ or _That's false._

A: _Irma is not writing._   A: _Van is sitting._

B: _That's true._   B: _That's false._

That's true.

3 Ask and answer questions about people's actions

A Study the form. Listen and underline the subjects and verbs. Notice the word order.
1-67

Information questions and answers	
A: What are you doing? **B:** I'm studying.	**A:** What are you doing? **B:** We're studying.
A: What is he doing? **B:** He's studying.	**A:** What are they doing? **B:** They're studying.

B Write the questions.

1. **A:** _____What is he doing_____ ?

   B: He's making copies.

2. **A:** _____ ?

   B: They're writing a report.

3. **A:** _____ ?

   B: He's getting coffee for the team.

4. **A:** _____ ?

   B: I'm writing questions.

5. **A:** _____ ?

   B: She's working at home.

6. **A:** _____ ?

   B: We're studying English.

C Listen to Jane talk to her manager, Ms. Green. Check (✓) the questions you hear.
1-68

1. a. ✓ What's happening? b. ____ What are you doing?

2. a. ✓ What's she doing? b. ____ What is he doing?

3. a. ____ What is it doing? b. ✓ What are they doing? *doing*

4. a. ✓ What is she doing? b. ____ What are they reading?

5. a. ____ What are we doing? b. ✓ What are you doing?

4 Ask and answer questions about your classmates' actions

Teamwork. Follow the directions with your classmates.

Student A: Act out an activity from the box or a different activity.

Student B: Ask the class: *"What's he doing?"* or *"What's she doing?"*

Classmates: Answer the question.

clean	read
cook	sleep
eat	wash the dishes
listen to music	watch TV
play a video game	write

▶▶ TEST YOURSELF

Close your book. Use your notebook. Write the answers to the questions: *What is your teacher doing? What are you and your classmates studying?* Compare your answers with a partner.

1 Listen to learn: paying utility bills online

A Look at the website title and vocabulary with your classmates. Which words are new to you?

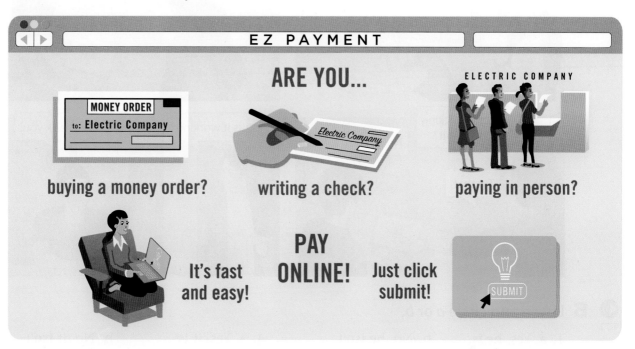

B Listen. Is this a news report or an advertisement? How do you know?

1-69

C Listen again. According to the speaker, which things are hard? Check (✓) the words.

1-69

- ☑ buy a money order
- ☒ click submit
- ☒ drive
- ☑ pay from home
- ☐ pay in person

- ☐ take the bus
- ☐ use a computer
- ☐ use a smart phone
- ☐ write a check

> **NEED HELP?**
>
> *I disagree with the speaker.*
> *I pay my bills in person.*
> *It isn't hard.*
>
> *I agree with the speaker.*
> *I don't like to buy money orders.*

D Discuss this question with your classmates: Do you agree or disagree with the speaker? Why?

2 Practice your pronunciation

A Listen for the stress in the words below.

1-70

    on<u>line</u>   sub<u>mit</u>   com<u>pu</u>ter   in <u>person</u>

B Say the words in 2A with a partner. Think about the stress.

3 Practice asking questions about a situation

A Listen and read the conversation. Who asks the questions? Who makes a suggestion?

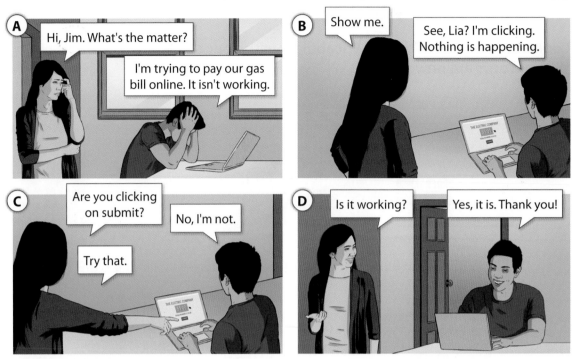

A Hi, Jim. What's the matter?

I'm trying to pay our gas bill online. It isn't working.

B Show me.

See, Lia? I'm clicking. Nothing is happening.

C Are you clicking on submit?

No, I'm not.

Try that.

D Is it working?

Yes, it is. Thank you!

B Listen and circle *a* or *b*.

1. a. Yes, he is.   (b.) No, he isn't.
2. a. Yes, she is.   (b.) No, she isn't.
3. (a.) Yes, he is.   b. No, he isn't.
4. a. Yes, it is.   (b.) No, it isn't.
5. (a.) Yes, she is.   b. No, she isn't.
6. (a.) Yes, it is.   b. No, it isn't.

C Think about the grammar. Look at the conversation and answer the questions.

1. How many questions do you see?
2. Name the verbs with *be + ing*.

D Work with a partner. Use the charts to make new questions and answers.

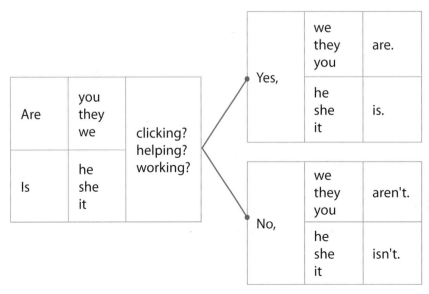

Are	you they we	clicking? helping? working?
Is	he she it	

Yes,

	we they you	are.
	he she it	is.

No,

	we they you	aren't.
	he she it	isn't.

4 Make conversation: paying online

A Work with a partner. Make a new conversation.

A: Hi, _____. What's the matter?

B: I'm trying to pay our _____ bill online. It isn't working.

A: Are you _____?

B: No, I'm not.

A: Try that!

B: Thanks! It's working now.

> **NEED HELP?**
>
> Types of bills
> gas
> electricity
> water
> power

B Present your conversation to another pair. Observe their conversation.

AT WORK ▶ Stating a problem and making suggestions

🔊 **A** Listen to the workers. What are the problems?

1-73

1. **A:** It isn't working.
   B: Try this.

2. **A:** It's broken.
   B: Let's fix it.

3. **A:** There's a problem.
   B: Let's look at the manual.

B Work with a partner. Take turns stating problems and making suggestions.

▶▶ TEST YOURSELF

Act out this situation with a classmate. Take turns with each role.

Student A: You have a problem. You don't know how to fix it.
Student B: You offer a solution to the problem.

1 Build reading strategies

A **Look at the pictures. Read the sentences. Who is using electricity?**

She is taking short showers.

She is doing laundry in the evening.

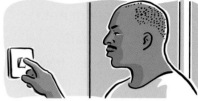

He is turning off the lights.

B **Preview the website below.**

1. Find the source. Where is this information?

   ☒ Oregon Department of Energy ☐ U.S. Department of Energy

2. Look for the date. Is this information current?

3. Look at the source, the title, and the pictures. What is the focus of the article? How do you know?

C **Read the website. How are people saving money on utilities?**

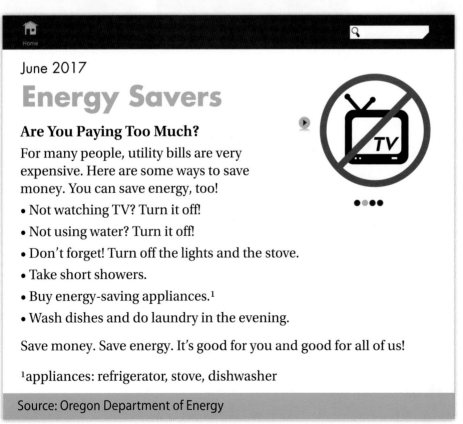

June 2017

Energy Savers

Are You Paying Too Much?

For many people, utility bills are very expensive. Here are some ways to save money. You can save energy, too!

- Not watching TV? Turn it off!
- Not using water? Turn it off!
- Don't forget! Turn off the lights and the stove.
- Take short showers.
- Buy energy-saving appliances.[1]
- Wash dishes and do laundry in the evening.

Save money. Save energy. It's good for you and good for all of us!

[1]appliances: refrigerator, stove, dishwasher

Source: Oregon Department of Energy

READER'S NOTE
Authors use bullets to mark important ideas.

D **Listen and read the website again. Do you do any of these things?**

1-74

E Read the questions. Fill in the bubble next to the correct answer.

1. According to the website, what is one way to save money?
   - (a) Turn off the TV.
   - (b) Eat lunch.
   - (c) Wash the dishes.

2. What is one way NOT to save money?
   - (a) Take short showers.
   - (b) Wash dishes at noon.
   - (c) Turn off the water.

3. Which things are appliances?
   - (a) stove, lights, refrigerator
   - (b) stove, dishwasher, refrigerator
   - (c) stove, TV, dishwasher

4. What did you learn from this article?
   - (a) ways to save money
   - (b) ways to save energy
   - (c) a and b

2 Read more about energy costs

A Look at the chart. What costs more: heating a home or heating water?

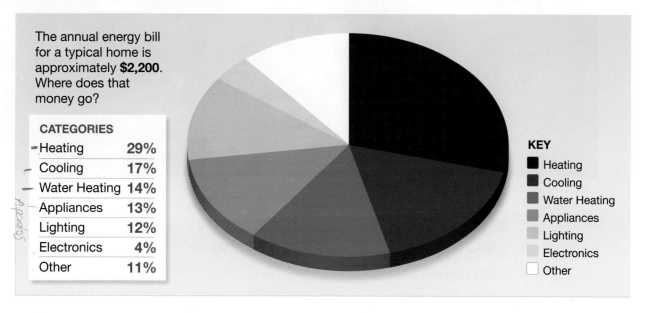

The annual energy bill for a typical home is approximately **$2,200**. Where does that money go?

CATEGORIES	
Heating	29%
Cooling	17%
Water Heating	14%
Appliances	13%
Lighting	12%
Electronics	4%
Other	11%

KEY
- Heating
- Cooling
- Water Heating
- Appliances
- Lighting
- Electronics
- Other

B Think about it. Talk about these questions with your classmates.

1. Think about different ways to save energy. Which are easy? Which are difficult?
2. List the types of energy your classroom or school uses. Is it too much? Why or why not?

⏻ BRING IT TO LIFE

Bring a utility bill from home or find one online. When is the payment due? Share your information with your classmates. Talk about whether you will pay online or by check.

A Work with a team. Look at the picture. Match the questions with the answers.

_c_ 1. Are they in the kitchen?

____ 2. What is Jan doing?

____ 3. Where is Katie?

____ 4. Is Bill playing with Katie?

____ 5. Is their TV small?

a. No, it isn't.

b. No, he isn't.

c. No, they aren't.

d. She's on the sofa.

e. She's reading.

B Work with a team. Write 6-7 new questions about the picture.

Who...? Is...? Where...? Are...? What...?

C Talk to people from other teams. Ask your questions.

D Work with your class. Write a paragraph about the picture.

Today is Saturday...

E Talk to your classmates. How can you save energy? Make a list.

Ways to Save Energy

Turning off the lights. _____ _____

Taking short showers. _____ _____

F Work with a partner. Use your list to make a chart. Then categorize the ideas from your list.

Easy	Difficult
Turn off the lights.	Buy an energy-saving appliance.

G Talk about your chart with your class.

PROBLEM SOLVING

A Listen and read about Mrs. Simms. What is the problem?

1-75

The Simms family is at home today. Mrs. Simms is cleaning the house. Her son, Jack, is listening to music. Her daughters, Judy and Joni, are watching TV. Mrs. Simms is tired. She's doing all the work.

B Work with your classmates. Answer the question.

What can Mrs. Simms do?

a. Play video games.

b. Tell the children to help.

c. Pay the children to help.

d. Other: _____

C Write Mrs. Simms a note.

Dear Mrs. Simms,

Here's something you can try: _____

_____ . I hope this helps you.

Sincerely,

_____

UNIT

5 In the Neighborhood

A LOOK AT
- Community
- *There is* and *there are*
- Giving directions

LESSON **1** VOCABULARY

AT WORK

1 Learn about places and occupations

A Show what you know. Circle the words you use.

1. school
2. convenience store
3. hospital
4. ambulance
5. EMT
6. bank
7. fire station
8. fire fighter
9. police station
10. police officer

B Listen and look at the map. What's on Elm Street?

2-02

C Listen and repeat the words from 1A.

2-03

D Write the vocabulary. Look at the map. Complete the sentences with the places you see. Then ask a partner: What places are in your neighborhood?

1. The children are at the _____school_____ .
2. The EMT and the ambulance are at the ___hospital___ .
3. The fire fighter is at the ___fire station___ .
4. The _____ , ___police station___ , and ___bank___ are on 1st Street.
5. The police officers are at the ___police station___ .
6. The ___convenience store___ , _____ , and _____ are on 2nd Street.

2 Talk about an intersection

A Work in a team. Match the words with the picture.

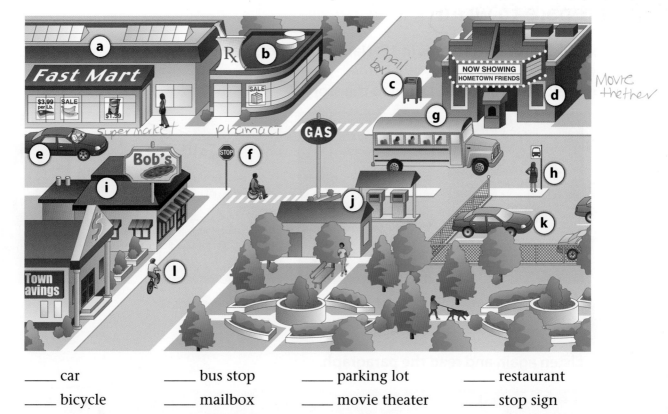

_____ car   _____ bus stop   _____ parking lot   _____ restaurant

_____ bicycle   _____ mailbox   _____ movie theater   _____ stop sign

_____ school bus   _____ gas station   _____ pharmacy   _a_ supermarket

B Listen and check your answers.

2-04

C Look at the picture in 2A and complete the chart with the transportation words. Read the sentences to your partner. Work together and make two new sentences.

Who?	Doing what?	Where?
A woman is	riding a _____	to the restaurant.
A man is	driving a _____	to the movie theater.
The children are	taking the _____	to school.

D Talk to a partner. Ask and answer questions about the pictures in 1A and 2A.

A: Where is the school?   A: What's the woman doing?

B: It's on 2nd Street.   B: She's going to the supermarket.

▶▶ **TEST YOURSELF**

Use your notebook. Copy this chart. Put words from the lesson in the chart.

Places	Transportation	Occupations

1 Prepare to write

A Talk about the pictures in 1B. Name the places you see.

B Look at the pictures. Listen to the story.

2-05

my apartment

my favorite
movie theater

my supermarket

me

C Listen again and read the paragraph.

2-05

My Neighborhood

Let me tell you about my new neighborhood. My apartment building is on 6th Street. It's next to a little library. There is a big park behind the library. My favorite movie theater is near my home. It's across from the post office. My supermarket is on Main Street between the bank and the clinic. There's a bus stop in front of my apartment. That's me. I'm waiting for the bus.

WRITER'S NOTE

Do two sentences have the same subject?

Use a pronoun in the second sentence.

<u>My apartment</u> is on 6th St. <u>*It's* next</u> to a library.

next to

behind

in front of

across from

between

D Check your understanding. Mark the sentences *T* (true) or *F* (false).

___F___ 1. There is a bank behind the library.

___T___ 2. His apartment is next to the library.

___T___ 3. The supermarket is on Main Street.

___F___ 4. The movie theater is across from the clinic.

___F___ 5. The bus stop is in front of the clinic.

E **Listen and complete the sentences.**

1. Alba's house <u>is on 4th Street</u> .
2. It's near <u>big park</u> .
3. There is a post office <u>next to the park</u>.
4. There is a bus stop <u>in front Post office</u>.
5. <u>Supermarket</u> is her favorite place in her neighborhood.

F **Compare your sentences with a partner. Listen again and check your work.**

2 Plan

A **Get ready to write. Use your notebook. Draw your house. Write the names of three places in your neighborhood.**

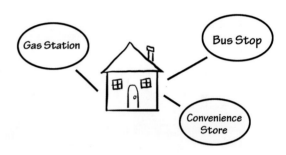

B **Talk about your drawing with your classmates. Ask: Is that a house or an apartment? What street is it on? What places are in your neighborhood?**

3 Write

A **Write a paragraph about your neighborhood. Complete the paragraph.**

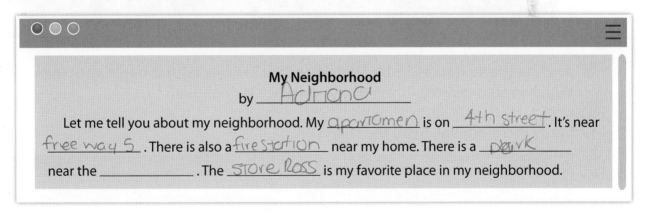

My Neighborhood
by <u>Adriana</u>

Let me tell you about my neighborhood. My <u>apartomen</u> is on <u>4th street</u>. It's near <u>free way 5</u>. There is also a <u>fire station</u> near my home. There is a <u>park</u> near the _____. The <u>store Ross</u> is my favorite place in my neighborhood.

B **Share your story. Read your paragraph to a partner.**

▶▶ TEST YOURSELF

Complete the following sentences. Share your responses with your teacher.

1. After this writing lesson, I can…
2. I need more help with…

1 Explore *there is* and *there are*: form and meaning

🔊 **A** **Listen and look at the picture. Read the story. Where is Dave?**
2-07

> My name is Dave. I live on 4th Street. There are two restaurants on my street.
> One restaurant is next to my apartment building. There's also a great supermarket.
> There aren't any movie theaters, but that's okay. There is a nice park across the
> street. Right now I'm sitting on a bench in the park. It's my favorite place to
> have lunch.

B **Analyze the sentences in 1A. Underline four sentences that begin with *there*.
Which sentences are plural? Which sentence is negative?**

C **Study the grammar. Read the charts.**

There is/There are	
Statements	**Negative statements**
There is a supermarket on 4th Street. There are two restaurants.	There isn't a post office. There aren't any schools.

D **Look at the picture in 1A. Change the sentences from false to true.**

1. There is one restaurant. ___F___
2. There's a movie theater. ___F___
3. There are two mailboxes. ___F___
4. There are two gas stations. ___F___
5. There aren't any people. _____

E Look at the picture on page 60. Write four sentences using *there is* and *there are*. Write two negative sentences and two positive sentences.

2 Practice: statements with *there is* and *there are*

A Listen to the sentences about the picture below. Circle *True* or *False*.

2-08

1. (True)   False
2. True   False

3. True   False
4. True   False

5. True   False
6. True   False

HILL STREET

B Look at the picture in 2A. Complete the sentences.

1. There __is not__ a convenience store next to the restaurant.
2. There __are__ some offices in the office building.
3. There __is not__ a mailbox across from the coffee shop.
4. There __is not__ a fire station on Hill Street.
5. There __are not__ any schools in the picture.
6. There __are__ places to eat.

GRAMMAR NOTE

a, some, any
Singular:
There is **a** bus stop.
There isn't **a** park.
Plural:
There are **some** restaurants.
There aren't **any** apartment buildings.

C Work with a partner. Talk about the pictures in 1A and 2A.

There is a _____ across from the ____Ross_____ .

There are some _____ .

There aren't any _____ on _____ Street.

3 Practice: ask and answer questions about a neighborhood

🔊 **A** Listen to the questions and answers. Underline the verbs. Notice the word order.
2-09

A: Is there a post office on Hill Street? **B:** Yes, there is.	**A:** Are there any restaurants on Hill Street? **B:** Yes, there are.
A: Is there a park on Hill Street? **B:** No, there isn't.	**A:** Are there any schools on Hill Street? **B:** No, there aren't.

🔊 **B** Listen to the answers. Write the questions
2-10

1. Is there a park on 4th Street? _____

2. Are there any people in the park? _____

3. _____

4. _____

> **GRAMMAR NOTE**
>
> Don't use contractions with *there are.*
> There are two banks.
>
> Don't use contractions with positive short answers.
> *Yes, there is.*   *Yes, there are.*

4 Ask questions about your classmates' neighborhoods

A Work with a team. Write one pair of questions for each member of your team. Choose from the places in the box or use your own ideas.

good restaurant	24-hour pharmacy	bus stops	library	office buildings

1. _____ _____ a _____ in your neighborhood?
2. _____ _____ any _____ in your neighborhood?

B Complete the chart with your questions. Talk to three people from other teams. Write their names and their answers on your chart.

Name: _____	Question 1: _____	Question 2: _____
1.	YES NO	YES NO
2.	YES NO	YES NO
3.	YES NO	YES NO

C Talk about your chart with your team.

There's a library in Kim's neighborhood. There isn't a library in Ivan's neighborhood.

▶▶ **TEST YOURSELF**

Close your book. Write three sentences about your school's neighborhood. Use *there is* and *there are.*

1 Listen to learn: giving directions

A **Look at the pictures. Read the directions.**

Go straight.

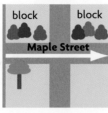
Go two blocks.

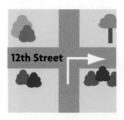
Turn right.

Turn left.

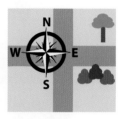
directions

2-11
B **Listen. Complete the directions to the clinic.**

1. Go _____*north*_____ on Grand Avenue.
2. Go _____ for one block.
3. Turn _____ on 12th St.
4. Go _____ on Maple St.

5. Go two _____ .
6. Turn _____ on 14th St.
7. Go _____ .
8. It's _____ the park.

2-11
C **Listen again and repeat.**

2 Practice your pronunciation

2-12
A **Listen to the sentences. Listen for the stressed words.**

1. The **police station** is in **front** of the **park**.
2. It's **across** from the **library**.
3. There's a **restaurant next** to the **movie theater**.
4. It's **behind** the **parking lot**.

2-13
B **Listen to the sentences. Underline the stressed words.**

1. There's a <u>park</u> <u>behind</u> the <u>fire station</u>.
2. The bank is next to the post office.
3. There are two restaurants on the street.
4. The bus stop is in front of the restaurant.

C **Read the sentences to a partner. Stress the underlined words.**

3 Practice asking for and giving directions

2-14 **A** Listen and read the conversation. Who asks for directions? Who gives directions?

A Excuse me. Is there a bank near here?

Yes, there is.

B Go up Main Street one block and turn left on 6th Avenue.

C Go past the clinic on the corner. The bank is next to it.

D Thanks for your help.

No problem. Bye!

2-15 **B** Listen and choose *a* or *b*.

1. a. a clinic   b. a bank   3. a. the bank   b. the clinic
2. a. Main St.   b. 6th Ave.   4. a. on the corner b. next to the clinic

C Think about the grammar. Look at the conversation and answer the questions.

1. What expressions with "go" does the woman use?
2. What word does she use after "turn"?

D Complete the sentences. Circle the correct words.

Go up Main Street.

Walk down Main St.

Drive past the park.

Walk across the park.

1. Go (past / right) the store.
2. Walk (up / in) Elm Street.
3. Turn (left / between) on Main St.

4. Walk (on the corner / across) the parking lot.
5. Drive (on / down) 2nd St.

E Work with a partner. Read the sentences in 3D.

68   Unit 5 Lesson 4

4 Make conversation: giving directions

A Work with a partner. Make a new conversation. Use the map on page 60.

A: Excuse me. _____ ?

B: Yes, there is. Go _____ .

Turn _____ on _____ .

The _____ is _____ .

A: Thanks.

B: No problem. _____ .

NEED HELP?

Ask for directions

Is there a bank near here?

I'm looking for a bank.

Is there one nearby?

B Present your conversation to another pair. Observe their conversation.

AT WORK ▷ Give directions inside a building

🔊
2-16

A Listen to the receptionist giving directions. Where does she work?

Take the elevator to the third floor.

Go down the hall.

It's the first door on the right.

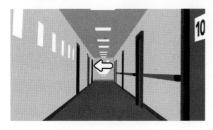

It's the last door on the left.

Go upstairs and turn left.

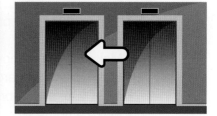

Go past the elevators.

B Work with a partner. Take turns asking for and giving directions in a building.

Excuse me. I'm looking for _____ .

▶▶ TEST YOURSELF

Work with a partner. Choose a situation. Act it out. Switch roles.

Situations: 1) In a neighborhood 2) At school

Student A: Ask for directions.
Student B: Give directions.

1 Build reading strategies

A Look at the pictures. Name the emergencies you see.

Home Emergencies

fire	power outage	accident	home emergency kit

B Work with your classmates. Make a list of items for a home emergency kit. Need more words? Ask your teacher or use a dictionary.

C Preview the website below. Look at the illustrations. What is one example of an emergency phone number? What is an emergency exit map?

D Read the website. Who can help in an emergency?

ABOUT   NEWS   BLOG   OUR STAFF   CONTACT US

Prepare for Emergencies

It's important to prepare for home emergencies. Here are some things to do:
- Make an emergency exit map of your home.
- Make a list of emergency phone numbers.
- Meet your neighbors. Neighbors can help in an emergency.
- Make a home emergency kit.
  Include: water, food, medicine, a flashlight, and batteries.

EXIT →

Emergency 911
Doctor 555-6262
Police 555-1394

READER'S NOTE
Illustrations, photos, and charts give you information about the text.

E Listen and read the website again. Are you prepared for an emergency?
2-17

F **Read the questions. Fill in the bubble next to the correct answer.**

1. To prepare for emergencies, _____ .
   ⓐ call the doctor.
   ⓑ write the doctor's phone number.

2. To prepare for emergencies, make _____ .
   ⓐ an exit map
   ⓑ a street map

3. To prepare for an emergency, meet _____ .
   ⓐ your doctor
   ⓑ your neighbors

4. <u>Include</u> water means:
   ⓐ put water in your home emergency kit.
   ⓑ put water in your kitchen.

5. Put _____ in your emergency kit.
   ⓐ a flashlight and batteries
   ⓑ pencils and paper

6. When is an emergency exit map important?
   ⓐ in a fire
   ⓑ in a power outage

2 Read an emergency exit map

A **Look at the emergency exit map. Answer the questions below.**

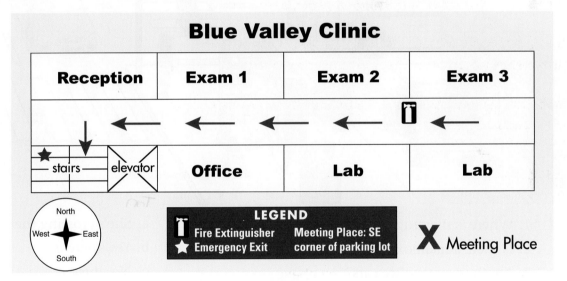

1. Is there an emergency exit in the building? _____
2. Are there any fire extinguishers in the office? _____
3. Do you take the elevator or go past the elevator? _____

B **Think about it. What's the best route to get out of your building? Work with your class. Write directions and draw an emergency exit map with the route.**

⏻ BRING IT TO LIFE

Work with your family or roommates at home. Make a home emergency exit map. Bring your map to class.

TEAMWORK & LANGUAGE REVIEW

A Work with a team. Look at the picture. Match the questions with the answers.

<u> d </u> 1. Where is the drugstore?

_____ 2. Is there a mailbox?

_____ 3. Are there any police cars?

_____ 4. What is the woman with the baby doing?

_____ 5. Is the restaurant next to the convenience store?

a. She's crossing the street.

b. Yes, there is.

c. No, it isn't.

d. It's on the corner.

e. No, there aren't.

B Work with a team. Write 5–7 new questions about the picture.

Is there…?   Are there…?   Where…?   What…?

C Talk to people from other teams. Ask your questions.

D Work with your class. Write a paragraph about the picture.

Let me tell you about this neighborhood…

E Interview three classmates. Ask: *Do you want a _____ near your home?* Check (✔) their *yes* answers in a chart like this:

park	police station	supermarket	fire station	hospital

F Discuss the data with your team.

Which places do most people want near their homes?

Which places *don't* most people want near their homes?

G Talk about the data with your class. Discuss reasons why people do or don't want these places near their homes.

PROBLEM SOLVING

🔊 2-18

A Listen and read about Jim. What is the problem?

> Jim is new in the neighborhood. His apartment is on Green Street. He is looking for the supermarket, but there's a problem with the directions. Jim is confused.

B Work with your classmates. Answer the question: *What can Jim do?* More than one answer is possible.

a. Go to a restaurant and eat.

b. Ask a neighbor for help.

c. Go home.

d. Other: _____

C Write Jim a text.

> Here's something you can try: _____
> _____
> I hope this is helpful!

UNIT 6 Daily Routines

LESSON 1 VOCABULARY

1 Learn everyday activity words

A Show what you know. Circle the words you use.

1. get up
2. get dressed
3. eat breakfast
4. take the kids to school
5. drive to work
6. pick up the kids
7. come home
8. make dinner
9. cook
10. wash dishes

🔊 2-19 **B** Listen and look at the pictures. What do they do after work?

6:00 a.m.

7:00 a.m.

7:30 a.m.

3:30 p.m.

4:00 p.m.

5:30 p.m.

6:30 p.m.

🔊 2-20 **C** Listen and repeat the words from 1A.

D Write the vocabulary. Look at the pictures. Write the words next to the times.

1. In the morning, they __get up__ , _____ and _____ breakfast.

2. Then, Brian drives _____ , and Jen takes the kids _____ .

3. Jen picks _____ the kids at 3:30 p.m., and they _____ home at 4:00 p.m.

4. In the evening, Jen makes _____ . She likes to _____ . After dinner, Brian washes
   _____ .

2 Talk about a daily routine

A Work in a team. Match the words with the pictures.

_____ do homework   _____ go to bed   _____ take a shower

_____ do housework   _____ have lunch   _a_ walk to school

_____ drink coffee   _____ ride the bus   _____ work

B Listen and check your answers. Then practice the words with a partner.

2-21

C Complete the sentences. Use the words in the box. Use your own information to write the times.

go	have	~~take~~	do	get	come

1. I _take_ a shower at _____ .   4. I _____ home at _____ .

2. I _____ dressed at _____ .   5. I _____ homework at _____ .

3. I _____ lunch at _____ .   6. I _____ to bed at _____ .

D Compare your sentences with a partner.

E Think about it. Ask and answer the questions with your classmates.

1. What is the best time of day to do homework? To do housework? Why?

2. Is it important to get up/go to bed at the same time every day? Why?

▶▶**TEST YOURSELF**

Use your notebook. Make a chart.
Put words from the lesson in the chart.
Use your own information.

Morning	Afternoon	Evening

1 **Prepare to write**

A Talk about the pictures below. Where does Tina work?

Good morning. Doctor's office.

> **WRITER'S NOTE**
> Use time expressions to make your writing clear:
> all day
> on Friday
> at noon

🔊 2-22 **B Look at the pictures. Listen to the paragraph.**

🔊 2-22 **C Listen again and read the paragraph.**

> **My Schedule**
> by Tina Aziz
>
>   My name is Tina Aziz. I work in a doctor's office. This is my work schedule. I work from 9 a.m. to 5 p.m., Monday to Thursday. I turn on the computer and the copy machine at 9:00. Then I check emails. I answer the phone all day. I also help the patients. I have lunch at noon. On Fridays, I don't work. It's my day off. I relax and take my kids to the park. I like my job a lot, but Friday is my favorite day.

D Check your understanding. Circle *a* or *b*.

1. Tina works _____ .
   a. four days a week   b. on Saturday

2. She answers the phone _____ .
   a. at 9 a.m.   b. all day

3. Tina has lunch _____ .
   a. at 11 a.m.   b. at 12 p.m.

4. She likes her job _____ .
   a. a lot   b. a little

🔊 2-23 **E Listen and complete the sentences about Mel.**

1. His name is Mel. He works at <u>a small market</u> .
2. He works _____ to _____ , from _____ to _____ .
3. _____ , he opens the door and turns on the lights.
4. He has lunch _____ .
5. _____ is his _____ . He relaxes.
6. He has dinner with _____ .

Mel at work

🔊 2-23 **F Compare sentences with your partner. Listen again and check your work.**

2 Plan

A Get ready to write. Complete the chart with your own information.

Morning	Afternoon	Day off
1.	1.	1.
2.	2.	2.

B Tell your classmates about your schedule.

In the morning, … In the afternoon, … On my day off, …

3 Write

A Write about your schedule. Complete the paragraph.

My Schedule

My name is _____ . I go to school at _____ . I go to class from _____ to _____ . I study _____ at school. On _____ , I relax. I _____ .

NEED HELP?

Ways to relax
go to the park
exercise
watch TV
listen to music
talk to family and friends
take a walk
play video games

B Share your paragraph. Read your paragraph to a partner.

▶▶ **TEST YOURSELF**

Complete the following sentences. Share your responses with your teacher.

1. After this writing lesson, I can…
2. I need more help with…

1 Explore the simple present: meaning and form

A **Look at the pictures. Read the sentences. What time does he leave work?**

He drives to work at 4 p.m.
He doesn't take the bus.

He turns on the lights in the
kitchen. He doesn't turn on the
lights in the dining area.

He cuts vegetables and makes
salads. He doesn't cook.

He leaves work at 10 p.m.
He exercises at home.
He doesn't go to a gym.

B **Analyze the sentences in 1A. Underline the verb in each sentence. What do you notice about the verbs? How are the positive verbs different from the negative verbs?**

C **Study the form. Read the charts.**

The Simple Present				
Statements				
I You	exercise.	We You		exercise.
He She	exercises.	They		

Negative statements				Contractions	
I You	do not exercise.	We You	do not exercise.	do not = don't I don't exercise. does not = doesn't He doesn't exercise.
He She	does not exercise.	They		

D **Work with a partner. Look at the charts in 1C. How many sentences can you make?**

2 Practice: talk about work routines

A Listen to the statements. Look at the pictures. Circle *a* or *b*.

1. a. Mina
   b. Alma

2. a. Pedro
   b. David

3. a. Delia
   b. Mina

4. a. Frank
   b. Pedro

5. a. Frank
   b. Pedro

6. a. Mina
   b. Alma

Mina types letters.

Frank repairs appliances.

David assists medical patients.

Alma waits on customers.

Delia makes copies.

Pedro programs computers.

B Look at the pictures in 2A. Circle the correct answers.

1. Frank (repair / repairs) appliances.
2. Mina (use / uses) a computer.
3. Mina and Delia (work / works) in an office.
4. Alma (doesn't / don't) work at a hospital.
5. David and Pedro (don't / doesn't) work at a restaurant.
6. Pedro doesn't (work / works) at a school. He (work / works) in an office.

C Talk to a partner. Follow the directions. Make true statements about the people in 2A.

A: *She works in an office.*
B: *Mina.*

3 Practice: ask and answer questions about schedules

🔊 **A** Listen to the questions and answers. Underline the simple present verbs. Notice the
2-25 difference between the questions and the answers.

Information questions and answers	
A: When do you work? **B:** I work five days a week.	**A:** When does he work? **B:** He works on Thursday and Friday.
A: When does she work? **B:** She works from 9 a.m. to 5 p.m.	**A:** When do they work? **B:** They work every day.

B Work with the grammar. Circle the correct word in the questions. Complete
the answers.

1. **A:** When (do / does) you get up?

   B: I _____ at 6:30 a.m.

2. **A:** When (do / does) they study?

   B: They _____ every day.

3. **A:** When does (you / she) exercise?

   B: She _____ in the morning.

4. **A:** When (do / does) Joe work?

   B: He _____ every weekend*.

5. **A:** When does Ruby (cook / cooks)?

   B: She _____ every evening.

6. **A:** When (do / does) you study?

   B: I study _____ .

   weekend = Saturday and Sunday

4 Ask and answer questions about your classmates' routines

A Work in a team. Write questions about routines.

Questions	Classmate's answers
What time do you _____ ?	
What time do you _____ ?	
When do you _____ ?	
When do you _____ ?	

B Talk to someone from another team. Write his or her answers in the chart.

C Talk about your answers and the answers in the chart with your team.

I get up at 6 a.m. Ruby gets up at 7:30 a.m.

▸▸ **TEST YOURSELF**

Close your book. Write three activities you do every day and three activities you don't do
every day.

1 Listen to learn: work routines

🔊 2-26 **A** Look at the pictures. Read the sentences and listen to the conversations. Then ask and answer the questions about your classroom.

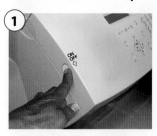 ①  ②  ③  ④

Turn on the printer. Push this button.

Turn off the computer. Push this button.

Fill the copy machine. Put the paper here.

Fill the stapler. Put the staples here.

1. Is there a copy machine?
2. Are there any computers?

3. Is there a printer?
4. How many staplers are there?

2 Practice your pronunciation

🔊 2-27 **A** Listen to the sentences. Listen for the verb endings.

s	She help**s** the principal.	He type**s** letters.	It print**s**.
z	She clean**s** offices.	He fill**s** the stapler.	It copie**s**.
iz	She fixe**s** computers.	He close**s** the store.	It use**s** staples.

B Read the sentences in the chart in 2A.

C Talk about Miguel's work routine. Practice the verb ending sounds.

He works at the supermarket. He opens the store.

 ① Supermarket OPEN

 ②

 ③

 ④ OPEN

 ⑤

 ⑥ CLOSED

3 Practice requesting help

A Listen and read the conversation. Which word means a problem?

B Listen and circle *a* or *b*.

1. a. the printer   b. help   3. a. help her   b. help Ken
2. a. no   b. yes   4. a. how to turn it on   b. how to put paper in it

C Think about the grammar. Look at the conversation. Find the word *help* three times. Notice the word after *help*.

D Study the grammar. Then work with a partner. Read the sentences. Make new sentences using object pronouns.

Singular		Plural	
Subject pronouns	**Object pronouns**	**Subject pronouns**	**Object pronouns**
I you he she it	me you him her it	we you they	us you them

1. Please help <u>Mary</u>.
2. Don't tell <u>John</u>.
3. Ask <u>Anita and Tim</u> for help.
4. Please give <u>Sara</u> the letter.
5. Can you help <u>the students</u>?
6. Tell <u>Mia</u> how to fill the stapler.

NEED HELP?

We often use object pronouns after these verbs: *tell, ask, help, give, show, call*

A Listen and read.
2-30

A: How can I help you, Mr. Glenn?

B: Can you show me how to turn on the computer?

A: Yes, of course. Just push this button.

B: Thanks for your help, Ms. Barns.

A: That's my job, Mr. Glenn. That's my job.

B Practice your conversation skills. Listen and repeat the questions.
2-31

Ask for help.

Hi. Can you help me?

Excuse me. Could you help me with the computer?

Could you show me how to fill the copy machine?

Offer help.

Can I help you?

How can I help you?

Do you need some help?

C Work with a partner. Make a new conversation.

A: Do you need some help?

B: Yes. _____ ?

A: Yes, of course. _____ .

B: _____ for your help, _____ .

A: _____ .

D Present your conversation to another pair. Observe their conversation.

▶▶ **TEST YOURSELF**

Act out this situation with a classmate. Take turns with each role.

Student A: Offer to help your partner with a problem.
Student B: Accept the offer. Ask for help with something in class. Thank your partner.

1 Build reading strategies

A Look at the pictures. Read the sentences. How much do you sleep every night?

He sleeps <u>a little</u>.

He sleeps <u>a lot</u>.

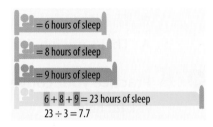

= 6 hours of sleep

= 8 hours of sleep

= 9 hours of sleep

6 + 8 + 9 = 23 hours of sleep
23 ÷ 3 = 7.7

On average, they sleep for 7.7 hours.

B Preview the reading

1. Find the source. Where is this information from?

   _____

2. Look at the title and read the first sentence. What is this article about?

   a. how people spend their time

   b. how people spend their money

READER'S NOTE
Use other words in the reading to help you understand new words. *On average, people <u>over 15</u> years old work for seven or eight hours.* In this sentence, *over 15* means *15 or more*.

C Read the article. How do people relax?

Where does the time go?

Many people in the U.S. work a lot and relax a little. Here's what people say about their daily routines:

On average, people over 15 years old work for seven or eight hours. They walk, drive, or ride to work for twenty-five minutes. They cook and do housework for about two hours every day. Then they have free time. They relax for three or four hours. They watch TV, exercise, spend time with friends and family, or read. They sleep for about eight hours.

Where does the time go? Now you know!

Source: United States Department of Labor

D Listen and read the article again.

2-32

E Read the questions. Circle the correct answers.

1. People sleep for _____ hours every day.

   a. six

   b. eight

2. Many people _____ for three or four hours every day.

   a. relax

   b. do housework

3. *About* eight hours means _____ hours every day.

   a. 9 or 10 hours

   b. 7.5 or 8.5 hours

4. People spend the most time _____ .

   a. cooking and doing housework

   b. working and sleeping

2 Read about housework

A Look at the chart. Then complete the sentences.

1. _____ cook and clean the kitchen for six hours every week.

2. Men work in the yard for _____ hours every week.

B Think about it. Talk about these questions with your classmates.

1. What kinds of housework do men do a lot? What do they do a little?

2. What kinds of housework do women do a lot? What do women do a little?

3. Who does the housework in your home?

C Work in a team. How much time do you spend on each activity? Find the averages for your team. Make a chart.

hours per week ÷ number of teammates

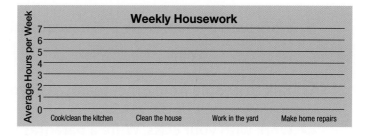

⏻ BRING IT TO LIFE

Search online for pictures of "clean the house," "clean the kitchen," "work in the yard," and "home repairs." Are there more men or women in the pictures? Talk about the pictures with your classmates.

A Work with a team. Look at the pictures of the Lim family. Match the questions with the answers.

__e__ 1. What time do Mr. and Mrs. Lim get up?

_____ 2. What does Mr. Lim do at 6:30 a.m.?

_____ 3. When does Mr. Lim take the kids to school?

_____ 4. What do they eat for dinner?

_____ 5. What does Mrs. Lim do in the evening?

a. At 7:30 a.m.

b. Rice, meat, and vegetables.

c. She checks her email.

d. He gets dressed.

e. At 6:00 a.m.

B Work with a team. Write 5–6 new questions about the pictures.

When…?   What…?   Where…?

C Talk to people from other teams. Ask your questions.

D Work with your class. Write a paragraph about the Lims' daily routines.

On most days, Mr. and Mrs. Lim…

E Interview three classmates. Ask: *What is your favorite part of the day? Why?*

Write your partners' names in a chart like this. Circle their favorite time of day. Take a note about why they like it.

Name	Favorite time of day
	morning afternoon evening
	morning afternoon evening
	morning afternoon evening

F Talk about the answers with your class.

Cai and Felipe like evenings because they like to sleep.

Sara likes mornings. She exercises in the morning.

PROBLEM SOLVING

2-33

A Listen and read about Nick. What is the problem?

Today is Nick's first day at his new job. He works at a bank. He answers the phones and works at a computer. Nick's manager says, "Make 100 copies and staple them for me." Nick doesn't understand the directions on the copy machine.

B Work with your classmates. Answer the question: What can Nick do?

a. Ask another person to make the copies.

b. Ask the manager for help.

c. Open and close all the copy machine doors.

d. Other: _____

C Work with your classmates. Make a list of things Nick can say.

Shop and Spend

A LOOK AT
- Shopping
- Simple present questions
- Making polite offers

LESSON **1** VOCABULARY

1 Learn about ways to pay

A Show what you know. Circle the words you use.

1. penny	3. dime	5. one-dollar bill	7. credit card	9. debit card
2. nickel	4. quarter	6. five-dollar bill	8. receipt	10. change

B Listen and look at the pictures. Are these things expensive?

2-34

C Listen again and repeat the words.

2-34

D Write the vocabulary. Look at the pictures. Complete the sentences.

1. The pencil is 25¢. Pay with a _____ .
2. The gum is 5¢. Pay with a _____ .
3. The candy is 10¢. Pay with a _____ .
4. The stamp is 1¢. Pay with a _____ .
5. Four quarters is _____ for a dollar.
6. Use a _____ to buy things online.
7. The book is $5. Pay with a _____ .
8. The coffee is $1. Pay with a _____ .
9. Use a _____ at the ATM.
10. Sign the credit-card _____ .

E Talk to a partner. What can you buy with a quarter? A one-dollar bill?
A five-dollar bill?

2 Talk about shopping

A Work together. Match the words with the pictures.

| ____ blouse | ____ dress | ____ pants | ____ shoes | ____ socks | ____ tie |
| ____ customer | ____ salesperson | ____ shirt | ____ skirt | ____ suit | ____ T-shirt |

B Listen and check your answers.

2-35

C Say and spell the words with a partner.

A: Can you spell blouse?　　B: Sure. It's B-L-O-U-S-E.

D Talk to a partner. Use the picture in 2A. Ask and answer questions about the clothes.

A: What color is the dress?　　A: How much are the pants?

B: It's blue.　　B: They're _____ .

E Think about it. Ask and answer the questions with your classmates.

1. What are you wearing today?

2. What are your favorite clothes?

3. Which is the best way to pay for clothes: cash or credit? Why?

▶▶ **TEST YOURSELF**

Use your notebook. Copy this chart. Put words from the lesson in the chart.

Cash	Ways to pay	Clothes

1 Prepare to write

A Talk about the pictures. Name the clothing items that you see. Discuss any words you don't know.

 B Look at the pictures. Listen to the story.

2-36

May I help you?

 C Listen again. Read the story.

2-36

A Trip to the Mall

It's cold this month, and I need a new sweater. When I want inexpensive, attractive clothes, I go to Dan's Discount Store. It's in the mall. Some stores in the mall are expensive, but Dan's has some great prices. It has a good selection of clothes for men and women. The salespeople are friendly, too. This weekend sweaters are on sale at Dan's. I usually pay with cash, but today I'm using my credit card.

WRITER'S NOTE

Use *but* to connect two sentences with different ideas.

D Check your understanding. Mark the sentences *T* (true) or *F* (false).

_____ 1. She needs a new shirt.

_____ 2. The clothes at Dan's are inexpensive and attractive.

_____ 3. The salespeople at Dan's are friendly.

_____ 4. The sweaters are expensive right now.

_____ 5. She's paying with cash today.

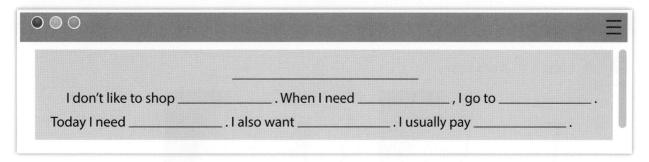

E **Listen and complete the sentences about Tom.**
2-37

1. Tom _doesn't like_ to shop at the mall.

2. He likes to shop at _____ .

3. Today he needs new _____ for work.

4. He also wants a new _____ .

5. He usually pays with his _____ , but today he is using _____ .

F **Compare sentences with your partner. Listen again and check your work.**
2-37

2 Plan

Get ready to write. Read and complete the chart with your classmates. Then circle the places you like to shop and the ways you like to pay.

Places to shop	Ways to pay
at discount stores	with cash
online	with a check

3 Write

A **Write a paragraph about yourself. Need help? Use the information in 2A.**

_____

I don't like to shop _____ . When I need _____ , I go to _____ .
Today I need _____ . I also want _____ . I usually pay _____ .

B **Share your story. Read your story to a partner.**

▶▶ TEST YOURSELF

Complete the following sentences. Share your responses with your teacher.

1. After this writing lesson, I can…
2. I need more help with…

1 Explore simple present *yes/no* questions: meaning and form

A Look at the pictures. How many people have jackets?

A: Do Jim and Joe have jackets?
B: Yes. They have new jackets.

A: Does Kathy have a jacket?
B: No, she doesn't. She
needs one.

A: Does Mario have a jacket?
B: Yes, he does, but he wants
a new one.

B Work with the grammar. Read the questions and answers in 1A. Circle the verbs. What differences do you see between the questions and the answers?

C Match the questions with the answers. Use the pictures in 1A.

_____ 1. Does Kathy have a shirt?   a. Yes, she does.

_____ 2. Do Jim and Joe need new jackets?   b. No, he doesn't.

_____ 3. Does Mario need a jacket?   c. No, they don't.

_____ 4. Does Kathy have a jacket?   d. No, she doesn't.

2 Practice: simple present *yes/no* questions

2-38

A Listen to Kai's story.

AT WORK

B Listen to questions about Kai's story. Circle *a* or *b*.

1. a. Yes, he does.   b. No, he doesn't.   4. a. Yes, they do.   b. No, they don't.

2. a. Yes, he does.   b. No, he doesn't.   5. a. Yes, he does.   b. No, he doesn't.

3. a. Yes, they do.   b. No, they don't.   6. a. Yes, he does.   b. No, he doesn't.

C Complete the questions and answers about Kai.

1. **A:** _____ have a white shirt?

   B: Yes, _____ .

2. **A:** _____ have new shoes?

   B: No, _____ .

3. **A:** _____ the salespeople at Super Discount wear brown shoes?

   B: No, _____ .

4. **A:** _____ wear black pants?

   B: Yes, they _____ .

5. **A:** _____ Kai need a vest?

   B: Yes, _____ .

D Work with a partner. Follow the directions. Ask and answer the questions in 2C. Then write two more questions about the pictures in 2A.

_____

_____

E Talk to three classmates. Ask and answer your questions.

3 Practice: talk about what people *have, need,* and *want*

A Study the grammar. Work with a partner. Use the charts to make sentences.

Statements with *have, need,* and *want*					
I You We They	have don't have	cash. new shoes. new socks. jewelry. a new uniform. a purple jacket.	He She	has doesn't have	a good job. a blue shirt. an expensive ring. a new purse. those sandals. a suit for work.
	need don't need			wants doesn't want	
	want don't want			needs doesn't need	

B Complete the paragraph. Circle the correct words.

1. Emily and Robert (are / have) shopping.

2. They (like / likes) the mall.

3. Today Emily (needs / want) new shoes.

4. She (want / wants) inexpensive brown shoes.

5. There (are / have) some nice brown shoes on sale for $25.

6. Emily (doesn't / isn't) have a credit card, but she (has / have) cash.

7. She (has / is) $40.

8. She (is / has) happy with her new shoes.

C Complete the questions about the paragraph in 3B. Then ask and answer the question with a partner.

1. _____ Robert and Emily like the mall?

2. What _____ Emily need?

3. _____ Emily want expensive shoes?

4. Does Emily _____ money?

5. Does Emily _____ her new shoes?

4 Ask and answer questions about clothes and shopping

A Work with a partner. Complete the questions. Add two questions.

Questions	Classmate's answers
Do you have a uniform?	
What do you wear at work?	
Do you need a new _____ ?	
Do you want a _____ ?	
_____ ?	
_____ ?	

B Interview a new partner. Write your partner's answers in the chart.

C Talk about the answers in the chart with your class.

Maria has new shoes.

▶ TEST YOURSELF

Write three sentences about your partner's answers from 4B.

My partner doesn't have a uniform. He wears a white shirt at work. He needs a new jacket.

1 Listen to learn: buying clothes

A Look at the clothing ad and complete the sentences below.

1. The _____ shirt is extra large (XL).
2. The _____ shirt is medium (M).
3. The _____ shirt is large (L).
4. The _____ shirt is small (S).

B Listen to the ad. When does the sale end?
2-40

C Listen again. Write the sale prices.
2-40

dresses _____   blouses _____   sneakers _____   sweatshirts _____

D Discuss this question with your classmates. Is it a good idea to get a new credit card at the sale? Why or why not?

2 Practice your pronunciation

A Listen to the numbers. Listen for the stress in each word.
2-41

| -teen | thir**teen** | four**teen** | fif**teen** | six**teen** | seven**teen** | eigh**teen** | nine**teen** |
| -ty | **thir**ty | **for**ty | **fif**ty | **six**ty | **seven**ty | **eigh**ty | **nine**ty |

B Listen and circle the prices you hear. Compare answers with a partner.
2-42

1. $15.00 $50.00
2. $60.00 $16.00
3. $40.28 $14.28
4. $12.16 $12.60
5. $10.18 $10.80
6. $6.19 $6.90

C Work with a partner. Say the prices in 1C and 2B.

3 Practice talking about things that are nearby or far from you

2-43

A Listen and read the conversation. What offer does the salesperson make?

2-44

B Listen and circle *a* or *b*.

1. a. Yes, it is.   b. No, it isn't.   4. a. Yes, she does.   b. No, she doesn't.
2. a. Yes, she does.   b. No, she doesn't.   5. a. Yes, she does.   b. No, she doesn't.
3. a. Yes, she does.   b. No, she doesn't.   6. a. Yes, she does.   b. No, she doesn't.

C Think about the grammar. Look at the conversation and answer the questions.

1. Find the word *this*. Is the customer near or far from the blouse?
2. Find the word *that*. Is the customer near or far from the blouse?
3. Are *this* and *that* singular or plural?

D Work with a partner. Study the grammar. Then ask and answer questions about things in the classroom using *this*, *that*, *these*, or *those*.

	near	far
singular	this	that
plural	these	those

A: What color is this pencil?   A: Is that door open?

B: It's yellow.   B: Yes, it is.

A: How much are these pens?   A: Do those students study English?

B: They're $1.00.   B: Yes, they do.

4 Make conversation: shopping

A Work with a partner. Make a new conversation.

A: Excuse me. _____ ?

B: It's on sale for _____ . What size do you _____ ?

A: I need _____ .

B: Here's a _____ in _____ . Would you like to try it on?

A: Yes, please.

NEED HELP?

Clothes

shirt

jacket

sweater

sweatshirt

T-shirt

B Present your conversation to another pair. Observe their conversation.

AT WORK ▸ Making a polite offer

🔊 2-45

A Listen to the employees. What does *Would you like…* mean?

Would you like to try on those pants?

Would you like to sit down?

Mr. Parr isn't here. Would you like to leave a message?

B Work with a partner. Say the offers in A. Then practice making other polite offers.

A: Would you like to _____ ?

B: Yes, thank you.

▸▸ TEST YOURSELF

Work with a partner.

Student A: You're the customer. Tell your partner what you want to buy.
Student B: You're the salesperson. Help the customer. Then change roles.

1 Build reading strategies

A **Look at the credit card statement.
Read the definitions.**

total amount due: everything you need
to pay

minimum payment: the amount you need
to pay now

interest: money that you pay for credit

B **Preview the article below and check the answers.**

1. Read the name of the website. What information can you find on this site?

☐ information about ways to pay

☐ information about places to shop

2. Read the title of the article. What do you think it's about?

☐ good things about banks

☐ good things about debit cards

> **READER'S NOTE**
> Website articles
> often have words
> that are links.
> These links take the
> reader to different
> pages or websites.

C **Read the article.**

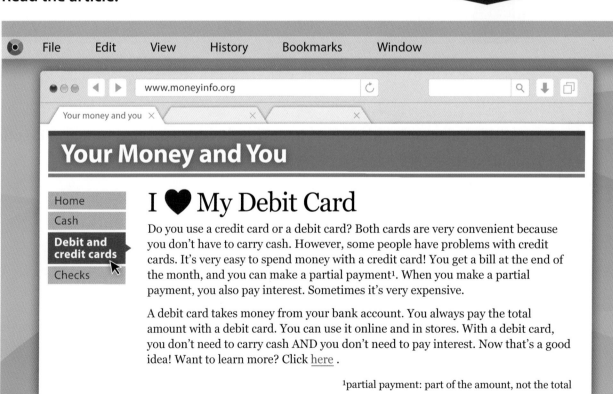

Your Money and You

I ♥ My Debit Card

Do you use a credit card or a debit card? Both cards are very convenient because you don't have to carry cash. However, some people have problems with credit cards. It's very easy to spend money with a credit card! You get a bill at the end of the month, and you can make a partial payment[1]. When you make a partial payment, you also pay interest. Sometimes it's very expensive.

A debit card takes money from your bank account. You always pay the total amount with a debit card. You can use it online and in stores. With a debit card, you don't need to carry cash AND you don't need to pay interest. Now that's a good idea! Want to learn more? Click here .

[1]partial payment: part of the amount, not the total

D **Listen and read the article again. Do you use a debit card?**
2-46

E Read the questions. Fill in the bubble next to the correct answer.

1. *Convenient* means:
   - ⓐ interesting
   - ⓑ easy to use
   - ⓒ fun

2. Credit cards _____ .
   - ⓐ use money from your bank account
   - ⓑ are not convenient
   - ⓒ are sometimes expensive

3. People pay interest when they _____ .
   - ⓐ make a partial payment
   - ⓑ use a debit card
   - ⓒ pay the total amount due

4. The writer likes debit cards because _____ .
   - ⓐ you pay once a month
   - ⓑ you don't pay interest
   - ⓒ you can make a partial payment

2 Learn about credit card interest

A Read the credit card interest calculator. Complete the sentences.

Total amount due: $1,000		Interest rate: 18%		
	Payment	Time to pay off[1] card	Total amount of interest you pay	Total amount you pay
Full Payment	$1000	1 month	$0	$1000
Partial Payment	$95	1 year	$97	$1097
Minimum Payment	$30	10 years	$799	$1799

[1]pay off = finish paying the total amount

1. Customer #1 pays $95 a month. He pays for _____ year. He pays $_____ in interest.

2. Customer #2 pays the minimum payment every month. He pays for _____ years. He pays $_____ in interest.

3. Customer #3 pays the total amount due. He pays $_____ in interest.

B Think about it. Talk about these questions with your classmates.

1. What kinds of purchases do people make with credit cards?
2. What happens when people make the minimum payment every month?
3. The author likes debit cards more than credit cards. Do you agree? Why or why not?

⏻ BRING IT TO LIFE

Go online. Search for "credit card interest rates." What percentages do you see? Share your information with the class.

A Work with a team. Look at the picture. Match the questions with the answers.

_c_ 1. What is Mrs. Kumar doing?

_____ 2. Does Mrs. Kumar like the green sweater?

_____ 3. Is the green sweater on sale?

_____ 4. Does Mrs. Kumar pay with a credit card?

_____ 5. Who are the sweaters for?

a. Yes, she does.

b. They're for her daughters.

c. She's shopping for sweaters.

d. Yes, it is.

e. No, she doesn't.

B Work with a team. Write 6–7 new questions about the picture.

Does...?   How much...?   What...?   Is...?   When...?

C Talk to people from other teams. Ask your questions.

D Work with your class. Write a paragraph about the picture.

Mrs. Kumar goes to the store.   The green sweaters .... She buys...

E Talk to your classmates. How can you save money when you shop?

> Ways to Save Money
>
> 1. _Shop at discount stores_
>
> 2. _____

F Work with a partner. Make a chart. Categorize the ideas from your list.

Shopping and Saving	
Do	Don't

PROBLEM SOLVING

2-47

A Listen and read about Joel. What is the problem?

> Joel is at the bank. He wants $40. He puts his card in the ATM. He takes his card, his money, and his receipt. When he counts the money, he only has $20!

B Work with your classmates. Answer the question: What can Joel do?

a. Call the police.

b. Put the card in the machine again.

c. Ask for help at the bank.

d. Other: _____

C Text Joel.

> Sorry to hear you have a problem.
> Try this: _____
> _____
> I hope this helps!

UNIT

8 Eating Well

A LOOK AT
- Food
- Frequency expressions
- Confirming information

LESSON **1** VOCABULARY

1 Learn food shopping words

A Show what you know. Circle the words you use.

1. fruit   3. basket   5. cart   7. cashier

2. vegetables   4. aisle   6. cash register 8. bagger

B Listen and look at the picture. Who is working at the store?

2-48

C Listen and repeat the words from 1A.

2-49

D Write the vocabulary. Look at the picture. Complete the sentences.

1. The _____vegetables_____ are between Aisle 2 and the fruit.

2. The _____ is next to the vegetables, on the left.

3. The _____ has a yellow tie.

4. The woman outside has a red _____ .

5. The man in white has a blue _____ .

6. The _____ has a green blouse.

7. The man in white is in _____ 2.

8. The cashier is using a _____ .

E Work with a partner. Talk about food shopping.

I buy fruits and vegetables every week. I use a cart. How about you?

2 Talk about a supermarket

A Work in a team. Match the words with the pictures.

_____ apples	_____ chicken	_____ lettuce	_____ potatoes
_a_ bananas	_____ eggs	_____ milk	_____ rice
_____ bread	_____ grapes	_____ onions	_____ tomatoes

2-50

B Listen and check your answers.

C Say and spell the words with a partner.

A: Can you spell _____ ?

B: Sure. It's __ __ __ __ __ __ __ __ .

D Talk to a partner. Talk about food shopping.

A: What do you buy every week?

B: I buy milk, eggs, bread, and fruit every week.

A: Where do you shop?

B: I shop at Amy's Market.

E Think about it. Ask and answer the questions with your classmates.

1. Where do you buy food?

2. Do you like small markets or supermarkets? Why?

▶▶ **TEST YOURSELF**

Copy the chart in your notebook. Complete it with words from the lesson.

Food	Things in a store	People in a store

1 Prepare to write

A **Look at the pictures. What's happening?**

B **Look at the pictures. Listen to the paragraph.**

2-51

oranges | chicken

C **Listen again and read the story.**

2-51

Going to the Supermarket

The Garcias make a shopping list every Wednesday night. They go to the supermarket every Thursday morning. Mr. Garcia loves oranges. They get oranges every time they shop.

Every week, they buy chicken, fish, and rice. Once or twice a month, they buy cookies or ice cream. They always look for good prices.

WRITER'S NOTE
Use commas for more than two things in a list.

D **Check your understanding. Mark the sentences _T_ (true) or _F_ (false).**

__T__ 1. The Garcias go to the market weekly.

____ 2. They make a shopping list on Mondays.

____ 3. They buy chicken every week.

____ 4. Mr. Garcia doesn't like oranges.

____ 5. They buy cookies every day.

____ 6. They always look for good prices.

🔊 2-52 **E** Listen and complete the sentences.

1. Brian goes to the supermarket _____ .

2. Every week, he buys _____ , _____ , and _____ .

3. He loves _____ .

4. He buys _____ and _____ every week.

🔊 2-52 **F** Compare sentences with your partner. Listen again and check your work.

2 Plan

A Get ready to write. Use your notebook. Write the answers.

1. When do you go to the supermarket?

2. List three things you buy every week.

3. List three of your favorite foods.

B Talk about your answers with a classmate. Ask questions about your partner's list.

Why do you go to the supermarket on _____ ?

Do you make a list?

Do you buy your favorite food every week? Why or why not?

3 Write about food shopping

A Write a paragraph in your notebook. Use your answers from 2A to help you.

Going to the Supermarket
I go to the supermarket every _____ . Every week, I buy _____ , _____ , and _____ . I love _____ . I always look for _____ .

B Edit your paragraph. Look for correct use of commas. Then read your paragraph to a partner.

▶▶ **TEST YOURSELF**

Complete the following sentences. Share your responses with your teacher.

1. After this writing lesson, I can…

2. I need more help with…

1 Explore frequency expressions

A **Read about Matt's work duties. Which words are new to you?**

Matt is a stock clerk at a small market. He cleans the aisles every day.

He unloads the delivery truck three times a week.

He makes new signs once a week.

Twice a year, he helps with inventory.

B **Analyze the sentences in 1A. Where is the frequency expression in most of the sentences? Can we put it at the beginning of the sentence?**

C **Study the form. Read the charts.**

Frequency expressions	
I cook	every day.
Mary goes shopping	once a week.
We buy cookies	twice a month.
They order pizza	three times a year.

More frequency expressions
every day / week / month / year
once a day / week / month / year
twice a day / week / month / year
three times a day / week / month / year

D **Look at Lucy's schedule. Complete the sentences.**

July 10-16

Sunday	Monday	Tuesday	Wednesday	Thursday	Friday	Saturday
	Cook dinner at home	Have dinner with Alex	Cook dinner at home	Cook dinner at home	Order pizza	Have dinner with Alex

1. Lucy orders pizza _____ .

2. Lucy has dinner with Alex _____ .

3. Lucy cooks dinner _____ .

E **Write three sentences about your schedule. Use frequency expressions.**

I cook dinner every night. I order pizza once a month.

2 Practice: questions and answers with *how often*

2-53

A Listen and look at the pictures. Complete Hector and Jane's schedules.

Job Duties
1. Hector
• check the aisles and put food on shelves
every morning
• unload the delivery truck _____
• make signs _____
• help with inventory _____

Job Duties
2. Jane
• check the aisles and put food on shelves
_____
• mop the floors _____
• clean the windows _____
• help with inventory _____

B Study the chart. Then look at the schedules in 2A and complete the questions.

Questions and answers with *How often*?	
A: How often does Hector check the aisles? **B:** Every day.	**A:** How often do they check the aisles? **B:** Twice a day. Hector checks the aisles every morning. Jane checks them every evening.

1. **A:** How _____ does Hector put food on the shelves?

   B: Every evening.

2. **A:** How often _____ Hector make signs?

   B: He makes signs once a month.

3. **A:** _____ Jane put food on the shelves?

   B: She puts food on the shelves every evening.

4. **A:** _____ Hector and Jane help with inventory?

   B: Three times a year.

C Talk to a partner. Ask and answer questions with *How often*. Use the schedules in 1A, 1D, and 2A.

A: *How often does Lucy cook dinner?*

B: *She cooks dinner three times a week.*

3 **Practice:** ask and answer questions about frequency

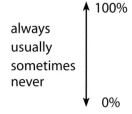

A Study the grammar. Listen and repeat the adverbs and the sentences.

2-54

> **Adverbs of Frequency**
>
> I **always** eat breakfast.
> I **usually** eat eggs for breakfast.
> I **sometimes** eat breakfast at home.
> I **never** eat pizza for breakfast.

↑ 100%

always
usually
sometimes
never

↓ 0%

B Work with the grammar. Circle the correct word.

1. I (usually / twice) cook in the evening.

2. She (always / once) buys apples.

3. They (three times / never) ride the bus.

4. Pat washes the windows (sometimes / once) a year.

5. They shop (always / once) a week.

C Match the sentences with the adverbs of frequency.

__a__ 1. I eat breakfast seven days a week.   a. always

_____ 2. Alicia eats at work three days a week.   b. usually

_____ 3. We eat at home six days a week.   c. sometimes

_____ 4. I eat pizza on Fridays.   d. never

_____ 5. Sam doesn't cook dinner.   e. once a week

4 **Ask and answer questions about your classmates' routines**

A Write another question in the chart. Interview two classmates. Write their answers.

Name:	_____	_____
1. How often do you order pizza?		
2. How often do you eat at a restaurant?		
3. How often do you cook at home?		
4. _____ ?		

B Talk about the answers in the chart with your class.

I order pizza once a month. Mia never orders pizza.

▸▸**TEST YOURSELF**

Write four sentences about your partner's answers from 4A.

Martin cooks dinner at home three times a week. He orders pizza once a week.

1 Listen to learn: food orders

A **Look at the menu. How much is a medium pizza with two toppings?**

PAPPA'S PIZZA PLACE

DRINKS:
SODA and ICED TEA
Small: $1.75
Medium: $2.25
Large: $2.75

PIZZA: Small: **$8.50** Medium: **$10.50**
Large: **$14.50** *Toppings: $2 ea.*

Pepperoni   Onion
Mushroom   Pepper

B **Listen and complete the orders.**
2-55

GUEST CHECK				
Date	Table	Guests	Server	128354

_____large pizzas
with onions
1_____ pizza with
pepperoni
_____ _____sodas

Total

Thank you! Please come again.

Guest Check				
Date	Table	Guests	Server	7742

_____ _____
pizza with peppers
_____ _____
iced teas
_____ _____
_____

Total

Thank you! Please come again.

GUEST CHECK				
Date	Table	Guests	Server	410121

_____ _____
pizzas with _____
and _____
_____small_____
_____ _____
_____

Total

Thank you! Please come again.

C **Discuss this question with your classmates.**

Would you like to work in a restaurant? Why or why not?

2 Practice your pronunciation

A **Listen to the questions and answers. What differences do you hear?**
2-56

A: Are you ready to order? ↗   **A:** Do you want anything to drink? ↗
B: Yes, I am. ↘   **B:** Yes, I do. ↘

B **Listen and circle *question* or *answer*.**
2-57

1. question   (answer)   3. question   answer   5. question   answer
2. question   answer   4. question   answer   6. question   answer

C **Work with a partner. Ask and answer the questions in 2A.**

3 Practice ordering food in a restaurant

A Listen and read the conversation. Is the employee polite?

2-58

Are you ready to order?

Yes, I am—a medium pizza with onions, please.

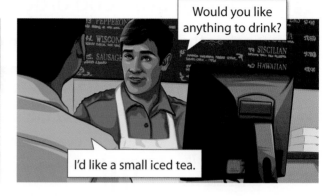

Would you like anything to drink?

I'd like a small iced tea.

Okay, that's one medium pizza with onions and a small iced tea?

That's right.

B Listen and circle *a* or *b*.

2-59

1. a. Yes, he is.
   b. No, he isn't.

2. a. Yes, he does.
   b. No, he doesn't.

3. a. Yes, he does.
   b. No, he doesn't.

4. a. Yes, he does.
   b. No, he doesn't.

C Think about the grammar. Look at the conversation and answer the questions.

1. What's another way to say, "Would you like anything to drink?"

2. What's another way to say, "I'd like a small soda"?

D Work with a partner. Read the grammar note. Then practice ordering the items below.

Questions and answers with *would like*	NOTE
Would you like anything else? Yes, I'd like a small iced tea.	*I'd = I would*

salad

a fruit salad

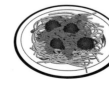

spaghetti

a bowl of soup

4 Make conversation: ordering food in a restaurant

A Work with a partner. Make a new conversation.

A: _____ ?

B: Yes, I am — _____ .

A: _____ anything to drink?

B: Yes, I'd like _____ .

A: Okay, that's _____ and _____ ?

B: That's right.

B Present your conversation to another pair. Observe their conversation.

AT WORK **Confirming information**

🔊 2-60 **A** Listen to the conversation. Why do the employees confirm the information?

That's onions, peppers, and mushrooms, right?

I'm sorry. What size?

The large one or the small one?

🔊 2-60 **B** Listen to the conversation again. Then practice with a partner.

A: I'd like _____ .

B: _____ ?

A: _____ .

▶▶ TEST YOURSELF

Work with a partner. Look at the menu on page 109.

Student A: Order a pizza and a drink.
Student B: Confirm the order. Then change roles.

1 Build reading strategies

A Look at the pictures and read the definitions. Name some healthy foods that you like. Do they have a lot of salt, sugar, fat, or oil?

| salt | sugar | animal fat | vegetable oil |

healthy: something that is good for your body

unhealthy: something that is not good for your body

B Preview the article. Read it quickly. Don't stop to look up words. Then answer this question. Why did the writer write this article?

☐ to teach about doctors and nutritionists

☐ to explain that people don't like fruits and vegetables

☐ to say that we need to eat a lot of fruits and vegetables

C Read the article. Why don't people eat more fruits and vegetables?

Doctors Recommend Fruits and Vegetables!

Doctors and nutritionists[1] say, "Eat a lot of fruits and vegetables every day." Fruits and vegetables are good for you because they have a lot of vitamins[2]. They don't have animal fat and they don't have added sugar or salt. Some people don't listen. They say, "Fruit is expensive," or, "I don't like vegetables."

Do you think fruit and vegetables are expensive? Look at the supermarket ads. Fruit and vegetables are on sale every week.

Do you eat the same fruit and vegetables every day? Try a new fruit. Eat a different vegetable. Find a new fruit or vegetable you like.

Listen to the doctors and the nutritionists. Don't eat a lot of unhealthy food. Eat fruit and vegetables every day and be healthy!

[1]nutritionist: a person who teaches, talks, and writes about healthy food

[2]vitamins: important nutrition

Source: *www.cdc.gov*

> **READER'S NOTE**
>
> Writers can use *because* to answer the question "Why?"
>
> *Fruits and vegetables are good for you **because** they have a lot of vitamins.*

D Listen and read the article again. Do you eat a lot of fruits and vegetables?

2-61

E Read the question. Fill in the bubble next to the correct answer.

1. "Doctors <u>recommend</u> fruits and vegetables" means _____ .

   ⓐ doctors say, "You like fruits and vegetables."

   ⓑ doctors say, "You need to eat fruits and vegetables."

   ⓒ doctors say, "You are eating fruits and vegetables."

2. Fruits and vegetables are good because _____ .

   ⓐ they aren't expensive

   ⓑ everyone likes to eat them

   ⓒ they are healthy

3. Why does writer say "eat a different vegetable"?

   ⓐ because they have different vitamins

   ⓑ because they have different amounts of salt

   ⓒ a and b

4. According to the writer, fruits and vegetables _____ .

   ⓐ are on sale every week

   ⓑ are expensive in some stores

   ⓒ have a lot of sugar

2 Read about recommended amounts

A Read the charts and answer the questions.

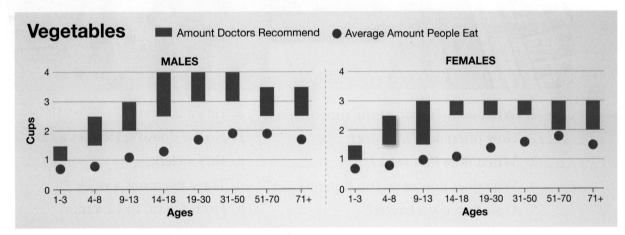

1. How many cups of vegetables do doctors recommend for 6-year-old boys? <u>1.5–2.5</u>

   How many cups do they eat? _____

2. How many cups of vegetables do doctors recommend for 25-year-old women? _____

   How many cups do they eat? _____

B Think about it. Talk about this question with your classmates.

A lot of people don't eat many vegetables. Why not?

 BRING IT TO LIFE

Look online. Use a search engine. Type the name of a food you like to eat + "nutritional information." Find out about the vitamins, salt, and fat content of the food. Share the information with your class.

ACADEMIC

A Work with a team. Listen and look at the picture. Then match the questions with the answers.

2-62

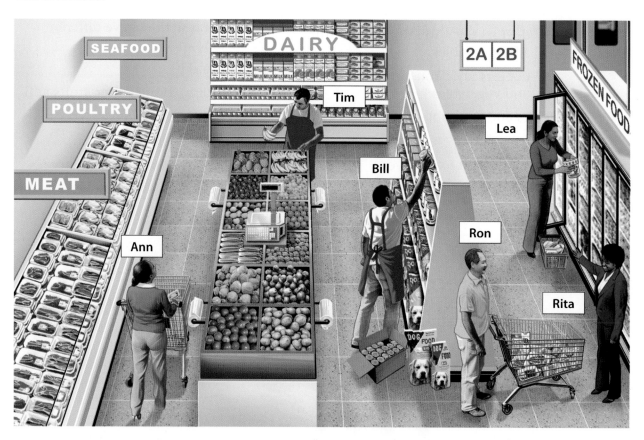

_____ 1. What does Tim do at the supermarket?

_____ 2. How often does he work?

_____ 3. When does Rita work?

_____ 4. Why does Ron go to the supermarket?

_____ 5. Does Ron use a basket?

a. He's a customer.

b. No, he doesn't. He uses a cart.

c. He's a clerk.

d. Three evenings a week.

e. From 4 p.m. to 12 a.m.

B Work with a team. Write 5-7 new questions about the picture.

How often...?   What...?   Where...?   Why...?   Does...?

C Talk to people from other teams. Ask your questions.

D Work with your class. Write a paragraph about someone in the picture.

Lea goes to the supermarket every Saturday. She buys...

E Interview three classmates. Write their answers in the chart.

Is your diet¹ healthy?			Why or Why not?
Name:	yes	no	I eat a lot of _____ . I don't usually eat _____ .
Name:	yes	no	I eat a lot of _____ . I don't usually eat _____ .
Name:	yes	no	I eat a lot of _____ . I don't usually eat _____ .

¹ diet = the food you eat

F Work with your class. Talk about the results. How do people improve their diets?

REAL-LIFE DATA

PROBLEM SOLVING

2-63

A Listen and read about the Ruzika family. What is the problem?

Sam and Lia Ruzika have two daughters. Every night at dinner the children say, "We don't like vegetables." Lia and Sam think, "Our girls need vegetables." Lia cooks different vegetables every night. She cooks broccoli, mushrooms, potatoes, and carrots. The girls never eat them. They say the same thing, "We don't like vegetables."

B Work with your classmates. Answer the question: What can Sam and Lia do? More than one answer is possible.

a. Order pizza with vegetables on it.

b. Tell the girls that vegetables are healthy.

c. Give the girls a lot of fruit.

d. Other: _____

C Write a list of things Sam and Lia can say to the girls.

1.	
2.	
3.	

UNIT

9 Your Health

A LOOK AT
- Health
- *Have to*
- Calling in sick

LESSON 1 VOCABULARY

1 Learn about parts of the body

A **Show what you know. Circle the words you use.**

1. head
2. nose
3. neck
4. back
5. chest
6. arm
7. hand
8. foot*
9. leg
10. knee

one foot / two feet

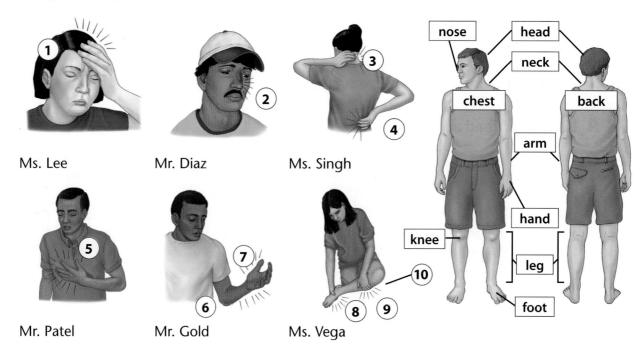

Ms. Lee   Mr. Diaz   Ms. Singh

nose   head   neck   chest   back   arm   knee   hand   leg   foot

Mr. Patel   Mr. Gold   Ms. Vega

 B **Listen and look at the pictures. Who are the people calling?**
3-02

 C **Listen and repeat the words from 1A.**
3-03

D **Write the vocabulary. Look at the pictures in 1A. Complete the sentences.**

1. Ms. Lee's _____ hurts.
2. Mr. Diaz's _____ hurts.
3. Mr. Patel's _____ hurts.
4. Ms. Singh's _____ and _____ hurt.
5. Mr. Gold's _____ and _____ hurt.
6. Ms. Vega's foot, knee, and _____ hurt.

E **Talk to a partner. Take turns.**

Student A: Say a part of the body.

Student B: Point to the part of your body.

2 Talk about a doctor's office

A Work in a team. Match the words with the picture.

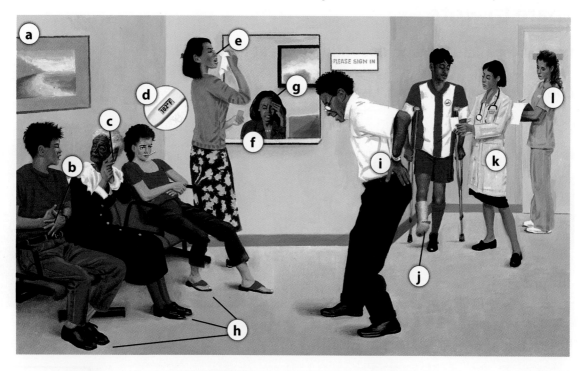

_____ backache   _____ doctor   _____ fever   _____ patients

_____ broken leg   _a_ doctor's office   _____ headache   _____ receptionist

_____ cold   _____ earache   _____ nurse   _____ stomachache

B Listen and check your answers.

3-04

C Say and spell the words with a partner.

A: Can you spell _____ ?   **B:** Sure. It's _____ .

D Talk to a partner. Ask and answer questions. Use the picture in 2A.

A: What's the matter with the man in the white shirt?

B: He has a backache. What's the matter with the receptionist?

A: Her head hurts. She has a headache.

E Think about it. Ask and answer the questions with your classmates.

1. What kinds of problems do people have with their backs? Feet? Stomachs?

2. What are some other illnesses you know about?

3. When do you go to the doctor?

▸▸**TEST YOURSELF**

Use your notebook. Make a chart.
Put words from the lesson in
the chart.

Parts of the body	Health problems	People

1 Prepare to write

A Look at the pictures. Who does Miguel see at the office?

🔊
3-05
B Look at the pictures again. Listen to the paragraph.

Your blood pressure is normal.

Miguel

🔊
3-05
C Listen again and read the paragraph.

> Miguel is at the doctor's office because he is sick today. He has a sore throat. First, he gives his insurance card to the receptionist in the waiting room. Then he goes into the examining room. The nurse takes his temperature and his blood pressure. After that, the doctor comes in. Miguel opens his mouth. The doctor examines him and writes a prescription. Miguel has to take his prescription medicine twice a day. Miguel has to stay home and rest. He wants to get well.

WRITER'S NOTE
Use words like *then* and *after that* to show what happens next.

D Check your understanding. Circle the correct word.

1. Miguel has a sore ((throat) / mouth).
2. Miguel needs his insurance (car / card).
3. The nurse takes his (temperature / medicine).
4. The doctor examines (him / a prescription).
5. Miguel has to take prescription medicine (once / twice) a day.
6. Miguel has to stay home and (rest / chest).

E Discuss the questions with your class.

1. What is a normal temperature?
2. What is a healthy blood pressure?
3. What information is on an insurance card?
4. What information is on a prescription?

F Listen and complete the sentences.

3-06

1. Ken has _____ .

2. First, the nurse takes his _____ .

3. Then the doctor _____ .

4. The doctor _____ for Ken.

5. Ken has to drink more fluids and

_____ .

Change your diet.

Drink fluids.

G Compare sentences with a classmate.
Listen again and check your work.

3-06

2 Plan

A Make a chart in your notebook. Complete
the chart with your classmates.

Job	Job Responsibilities
receptionist	
nurse	
doctor	

3 Write

A Write a paragraph in your notebook. Use the chart in 2A to help you.

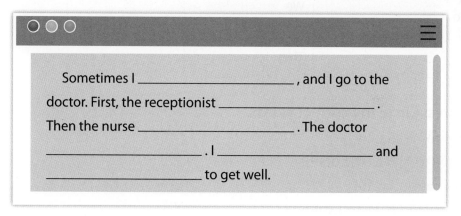

Sometimes I _____ , and I go to the
doctor. First, the receptionist _____ .
Then the nurse _____ . The doctor
_____ . I _____ and
_____ to get well.

NEED HELP?

Ways to get well
stay home
rest
take medicine
drink fluids

B Edit your paragraph. Look for correct use of *then* or *after that*. Then read your
paragraph to a partner.

⯈⯈ **TEST YOURSELF**

Complete the following sentences. Share your responses with your teacher.

1. After this writing lesson, I can…
2. I need more help with…

1 Explore *have to*: meaning and form

A **Look at the pictures. Read the sentences. Where does Jeff have to go?**

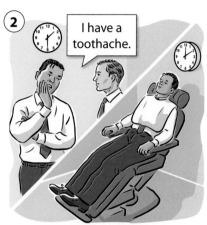

Maria has to leave class early.
She has to pick up her son.

Jeff has to leave work early.
He has to go to the dentist.

Kim and Rosa have to leave
the party early. They have to
study.

B **Work with the grammar. Read the questions and answers in 1A. Underline *have to/has to* + verb in each sentence. What do you notice about the verbs?**

C **Study the form. Read the charts.**

Statements with *have to*					
I You	have to	go to the dentist.	We You	have to	go to the dentist.
He She	has to		They		

D **Look at the pictures. Circle the correct words.**

1. Maria (has / has to) a son.

2. Jeff (has to / have to) go to the dentist.

3. He (has to / has) a toothache.

4. Kim and Rose (has to / have to) study.

5. They (have / have to) a test tomorrow.

6. They (have / have to) leave early.

E **Talk to a partner. Talk about things you have to do this week.**

A: *I have to study. How about you?*

B: *I have to go to the bank.*

2 Practice: statements with *have to*

3-07

A Listen to the sentences about the picture. Circle *True* or *False*.

1. True	False	3. True	False	5. True	False
2. True	False	4. True	False	6. True	False

B Look at the picture in 2A. Circle the correct words.

1. Bill (has / has to) high blood pressure. He (has to / have to) exercise.

2. Jake (has / has to) a cold. He has (to / a) take medicine and (rest / play).

3. Mike (has / has to) high blood pressure. He (has / has to) quit smoking.

4. Wilma (like / likes) coffee and donuts, but she (has / have) to change her diet.

5. Maria (isn't / hasn't) at work today. She (has to / like to) stay home with her sick son.

C Talk to a partner. Follow the directions.

Student A: Make true and false statements about the picture in 2A.

Student B: Say: *That's true.* or *That's false.* Then make a true statement.

A: *Wilma likes to drink coffee.*　　　　　　　　**A:** *Jake has to quit smoking.*

B: *That's true. Wilma likes to drink coffee.*　　**B:** *That's false. Mike has to quit smoking.*

D Look at the picture on page 117. Write sentences about two of the people. Use *have* and *have to*.

The woman has a cold. She has to drink fluids.

3 Practice: ask and answer questions with *have to*

A Study the grammar. Listen to the questions and answers. Underline the complete verb in each question. How many parts does it have?

3-08

Information questions and answers with *have to*	
A: Why do you have to leave early? **B:** I have to pick up my children.	**A:** Why does he have to leave early? **B:** He has to go to the doctor.
A: Why do they have to leave early? **B:** They have to study.	**A:** Why does she have to leave early? **B:** She has to go to the dentist.

B Work with the grammar. Match the questions with the answers.

_____ 1. Why do you have to leave early?

_____ 2. Why does Jeff have to go to the dentist?

_____ 3. Why does Maria have to talk to the teacher?

_____ 4. Why do the girls have to go to the library?

_____ 5. Why does Miguel have to see the doctor?

a. She has to leave early.

b. He has a sore throat.

c. They have to study.

d. I have to pick up my son.

e. He has a toothache.

4 Ask and answer questions about your day

A Complete the questions with the words in the box. Then answer the questions with your own information.

~~Why~~ What When Where

1. _Why_ do you have to come to class every day? _____

2. _____ do you have to do after class today? _____

3. _____ do you have to go after class? _____

4. _____ do you have to get up tomorrow? _____

B Talk to three classmates. Ask and answer the questions. Then write four sentences about your classmates.

Teresa has to practice English. Tran has to go home after class. Ana has to make lunch for her family. Milo has to get up at 8:15 tomorrow.

▶▶ **TEST YOURSELF**

Close your book. Write five things you have to do this week. Use complete sentences.

1 Listen to learn: going to the doctor

🔊 3-09 **A** Listen to the radio program. Check the symptoms you hear.

☐ fever

☐ headache

☐ congestion

☐ sore throat

☐ cough

🔊 3-09 **B** Listen again. Check the speaker's advice.

1. a fever	☐ stay home	☐ call the doctor
2. a bad sore throat	☐ stay home	☐ call the doctor
3. a cold	☐ stay home	☐ call the doctor
4. a high fever	☐ stay home	☐ call the doctor

C Discuss this question: Do you agree with the speaker? When do you stay home/ call the doctor?

2 Practice your pronunciation

🔊 3-10 **A** Listen to the sentences. Listen to the difference between *have to/have* and *has to/has.*

I **have to** see the doctor.   She **has to** go at 2:30.

I **have** a cold.   She **has** a new job.

🔊 3-11 **B** Listen and circle the words you hear. Then listen again and repeat the sentences.

1. have to   have   3. has to   has

2. have to   has to   4. have   has

3 Practice making an appointment

A Listen and read the conversation.

3-12

Hello, doctor's office.

Hi. This is Carl. I have a terrible cold. I have to see the doctor.

I'm sorry but I don't have any openings today. Is tomorrow OK?

OK.

How about 10 a.m.?

That's fine. Thanks.

OK. See you on Wednesday, May 12th at 10:00.

B Listen and circle *a* or *b*.

3-13

1. a. He has a fever.   b. He has a cold.   3. a. on Wednesday   b. on Thursday

2. a. Yes, it is.   b. No, it isn't.   4. a. at 10:00   b. at 2:00

C Think about the grammar. Look at the conversation. When do we use *on* and *at*?

D Study the grammar. Listen and repeat the sentences.

3-14

At	On
I have to leave at 5:00.	We have to work on Wednesday.
She has class at 11:30.	He has an appointment on March 10th.

E Listen and complete the appointment cards.

3-15

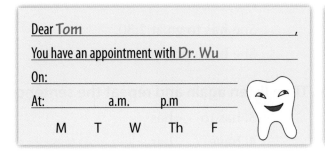

Dear Tom _____,
You have an appointment with Dr. Wu _____
On: _____
At: _____ a.m. _____ p.m _____
M   T   W   Th   F

Dear _____,
You have an appointment with _____
On: _____
At: _____ a.m. _____ p.m _____
M   T   W   Th   F

F Talk to a partner. Make statements about the appointment cards.

Tom has to see the dentist on Tuesday.

4 Make conversation: making an appointment

A Work with a partner. Make a new conversation. Use your own ideas.

A: Hello, _____ 's office.

B: Hello. This is _____ . I have a _____ . I have to see the _____ .

A: Let's see. I have an opening on _____ . Is that OK?

B: Yes, _____ . Thanks.

A: Okay. See you _____ .

B Present your conversation to another pair. Observe their conversation.

AT WORK ▶ Calling in sick

🔊 **A** Listen to the employees. What does *definitely* mean?
3-16

A: This is Carla Lopez. My son is sick and I have to take him to the doctor.

B: Are you coming in tomorrow?

A: Yes, definitely.

A: This is Mark. I'm sorry, but I can't come in today. I have a fever.

B: If you're not well tomorrow, call again.

A: Of course.

B Work with a partner. Read the conversations in A. Then practice calling in sick. Use your own ideas. Take turns.

▶▶ **TEST YOURSELF**

Act out this situation with a classmate. Take turns.

Student A: You're the patient. Make an appointment.
Student B: You're the receptionist.

1 Build reading strategies

A Read the definitions. Can you name an over-the-counter medicine?

checkup: a medical examination to check your health when you are not sick.

over-the-counter medicine: medicine you don't need a prescription to buy.

B Preview the reading. Circle the answers.

1. What is the title of the article?

    a. Feeling Fine   b. Staying Well   c. Taking Medicine   d. a, b, and c

2. What is the article about?

    a. staying well   b. taking medicine   c. choosing a doctor   d. a and b

C Read the article.

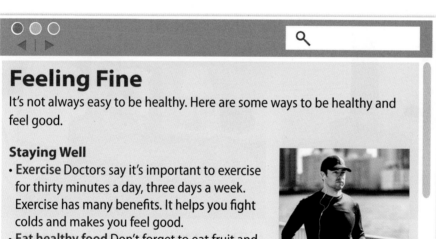

Feeling Fine

It's not always easy to be healthy. Here are some ways to be healthy and feel good.

Staying Well
- **Exercise** Doctors say it's important to exercise for thirty minutes a day, three days a week. Exercise has many benefits. It helps you fight colds and makes you feel good.
- **Eat healthy food** Don't forget to eat fruit and vegetables every day. They're good for you, and they taste good.
- **Have regular checkups** See your doctor for a checkup once a year. Always follow your doctor's health instructions.

Taking Medicine
If you feel sick, you can take over-the-counter medicine. Sometimes over-the-counter medicine helps people feel better. It's important to read and follow the directions exactly.[1] Over-the-counter medicines don't always stop the problem. Then you have to go to the doctor.

[1]exactly = with no mistakes

READER'S NOTE
The headings of an article tell you what each part is about. This article has two headings: *Staying Well* and *Taking Medicine*.

 D Listen and read the article in 1C again. What do you do to stay well?
3-17

E **Read the questions. Fill in the bubble next to the correct answer.**

1. *Benefits* means _____ .
   ⓐ good things
   ⓑ problems
   ⓒ difficulties

2. According to the writer, you need a checkup _____ .
   ⓐ every month
   ⓑ twice a year
   ⓒ once a year

3. The article says that it's important to _____ .
   ⓐ buy over-the-counter medicine
   ⓑ read directions on medicine carefully
   ⓒ get prescription medicine from the doctor

4. The article says over-the-counter medicine _____ .
   ⓐ doesn't work sometimes
   ⓑ is not a good idea
   ⓒ is too expensive for many people

2 Read directions and warnings on medicine labels.

A **Read the medicine labels. Match the sentences with the labels.**

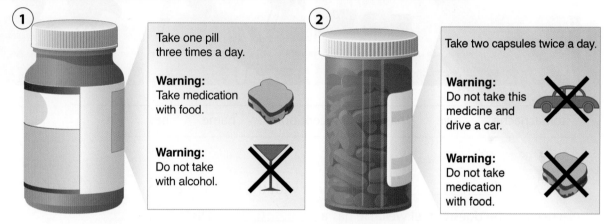

1 Take one pill three times a day.

Warning: Take medication with food.

Warning: Do not take with alcohol.

2 Take two capsules twice a day.

Warning: Do not take this medicine and drive a car.

Warning: Do not take medication with food.

1. Do not take this medicine and drive a car. ____
2. Take this medicine with food. ____
3. Do not take this with alcohol. ____
4. Take this medicine twice a day. ____
5. Do not take this with food. ____
6. Take this medicine three times a day. ____

B **Think about it. Talk about the questions with your classmates.**

1. What other warnings are on medicine labels? Name or draw two other warnings you know.

2. What do you do if you don't understand a medicine label?

⏻ BRING IT TO LIFE

Look at a medicine label online. Write the name of the medicine. Draw or copy the warning labels. Share the information with your classmates.

A Work with a team. Look at the picture. Use the words in the box to complete the beginning of the story.

Health Form

Name: *Andre Zolmar*
Date of birth: *July 8, 1983*
Current symptoms: *stomachache*

Health History:

Childhood Diseases:

☑ chicken pox
☑ diphtheria
☑ rubella
☑ measles
☐ mumps
☐ other

stomachache	give	has to	receptionist	name	~~has~~	at

Andre _____has_____ an appointment with the doctor today because he doesn't feel well. He has a _____ . His appointment is _____ 2:00. He arrives early. When he gets to the waiting room, he has to _____ his insurance card to the _____ . He also _____ complete a health form. He writes his _____ and his symptoms on the form.

B Work with a team. Continue the story.

Andre goes into the examining room. …

C Share your story with another team.

D Work with your class. Write four questions and answers about the pictures in A.

Why…?   When…?   What…?

E Work with a partner. How can you stay healthy? If you're sick, how can you get well? Write the ideas in a chart.

Stay healthy	Get well
wash your hands	rest

F Work with your class. Share your chart and add more ideas.

G Talk to your classmates. Discuss the ideas in your chart.

1. Which ones do you always do?

2. Which ones do you sometimes do?

3. Why *don't* people do some of these things?

PROBLEM SOLVING

3-18

A Listen and read about David. What is the problem?

David teaches English in the evening. He likes his job and his students very much. Every day he tells his students, "You have to come to school every day. Don't stay home! Come and learn English every day." David has a problem today. He has a terrible headache and a stomachache too. He doesn't want to go home, but he feels terrible.

B Work with your classmates. Answer the question: What can David do? (More than one answer is possible.)

a. Call the doctor.

b. Go home now.

c. Stay at school now, but stay home tomorrow.

d. Other: _____

C Write a note for David to give his students.

Dear students,

I'm sorry, but I have to _____. Don't forget: Come _____ !

See you soon,

David

UNIT
10 Getting the Job

A LOOK AT
■ Jobs
■ Simple past with *be*
■ Job interview skills

LESSON **1** VOCABULARY

1 Learn names of jobs

A Show what you know. Which people work in healthcare?

repair

1. computer technician
2. auto mechanic

take care of

3. childcare worker
4. home health aide

help

5. physician's assistant
6. dental assistant

B Listen and look at the pictures. Which people like their jobs?
3-19

C Listen and repeat the words from 1A.
3-20

D Write the vocabulary. Look at the pictures. Complete the sentences.

1. The <u>home health aide</u> works in people's homes. She takes care of elderly people.
2. The _____ repairs cars. He works in a garage.
3. The _____ works in an office. He repairs computers.
4. The _____ works at a hospital. He helps the doctors.
5. The _____ works in a dentist's office. She helps the dentist.
6. The _____ works at a daycare center. She takes care of children.

2 Talk about jobs and skills

A Work in a team. Match the words with the picture.

_____ busser   _a_ delivery person   _____ manager   _____ plumber

_____ cook   _____ gardener   _____ painter   _____ server

B Listen and check your answers. Then practice the words with a partner.

3-21

C Ask and answer questions about jobs. Use the words in the box.

| cleans tables | cooks food | works in gardens | paints buildings |
| delivers packages | manages a business | serves food | repairs |

A: What does a plumber do?

B: A plumber repairs sinks.

D Think about it. Ask and answer the questions with your classmates.

1. What are some jobs at a school? At a supermarket? At a shopping mall?

2. What job skills does a childcare worker need?

3. What are some job skills you need?

▶▶ TEST YOURSELF

Use your notebook. Copy this chart.
Put words from the lesson in the chart.

Jobs	Job skills

1 Prepare to write

A Look at the job ads and listen to the email. What job is Sergei applying for?

3-22

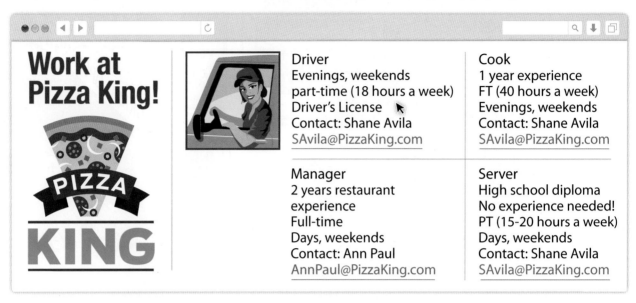

Work at Pizza King!

Driver
Evenings, weekends
part-time (18 hours a week)
Driver's License
Contact: Shane Avila
SAvila@PizzaKing.com

Cook
1 year experience
FT (40 hours a week)
Evenings, weekends
Contact: Shane Avila
SAvila@PizzaKing.com

Manager
2 years restaurant experience
Full-time
Days, weekends
Contact: Ann Paul
AnnPaul@PizzaKing.com

Server
High school diploma
No experience needed!
PT (15-20 hours a week)
Days, weekends
Contact: Shane Avila
SAvila@PizzaKing.com

B Listen again. Read the email.

3-22

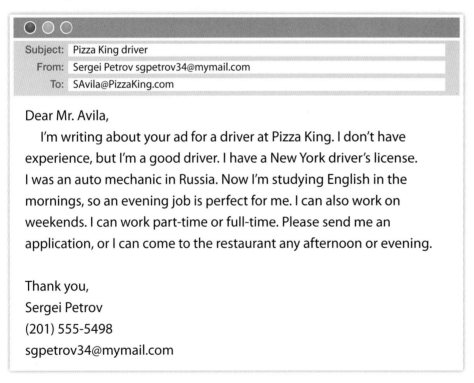

Subject: Pizza King driver
From: Sergei Petrov sgpetrov34@mymail.com
To: SAvila@PizzaKing.com

Dear Mr. Avila,

I'm writing about your ad for a driver at Pizza King. I don't have experience, but I'm a good driver. I have a New York driver's license. I was an auto mechanic in Russia. Now I'm studying English in the mornings, so an evening job is perfect for me. I can also work on weekends. I can work part-time or full-time. Please send me an application, or I can come to the restaurant any afternoon or evening.

Thank you,
Sergei Petrov
(201) 555-5498
sgpetrov34@mymail.com

WRITER'S NOTE
When you send an email about a job, put your contact information at the end.

C Check your understanding. Mark the sentences *T* (true) or *F* (false).

_____ 1. Sergei wants the driver job.

_____ 2. He lives in Russia now.

_____ 3. He is a pharmacist in New York.

_____ 4. He can work in the mornings.

_____ 5. He can work on Saturday.

_____ 6. He has the job application.

D Listen and complete the sentences.

1. She is writing about the ad for a _____ .

2. She has a _____ .

3. She can work _____ .

4. Please send her _____ .

E Compare sentences with a partner. Listen again and check your work.

2 Plan

A Get ready to write. Complete the chart. Choose a job from 1A or your own idea.

Job title:	Days you can work:	Times you can work:	Full-time or part-time:

B Share your chart with a partner. Talk about the jobs you want and when you can work.

3 Write

A Write an email to an employer.

Dear _____ ,

    I'm writing about your ad for a _____ . I can work _____ . I can also work _____ . Please send me _____ .

Thank you,

_____

_____

_____

B Edit your email. Check your contact information. Then read your email to a partner.

▶▶ **TEST YOURSELF**

Complete the following sentences. Share your response with your teacher.

1. After this writing lesson, I can…

2. I need more help with…

1 Explore the simple past with *be*: meaning and form

A Look at the pictures. Was Rico a farmer or a gardener in 2005?

1995–2005
Rico was a farmer.

2006–2008
He was a student.

2009–2013
He was a gardener.

2013–present
Now he is a business owner.

B Analyze the sentences in 1A. Which one has a different verb form? Why is it different?

C Study the form. Read the charts.

Statements

I	was	a gardener. a student. a cook.	We	were	gardeners. students. cooks.
You	were		You		
He She	was		They		

Negative statements

I	was not	a gardener. a student. a cook.	We	were not	gardeners. students. cooks.
You	were not		You		
He She	was not		They		

Contractions

was not = wasn't
I wasn't a gardener.

were not = weren't
They weren't gardeners.

D Work with a partner. Look at the charts in 1C. Take turns making sentences.

2 Practice the simple past with *be*

A Listen to the statements about the pictures. Circle the correct answers.

Sofia | Emily

1998

Sofia / Emily

2003

Sofia / Emily

2011

Sofia / Emily

2016

Sofia | Emily

1. a. Emily   b. Sofia   (c.) Emily and Sofia

2. a. Emily   b. Sofia   c. Emily and Sofia

3. a. Emily   b. Sofia   c. Emily and Sofia

4. a. Emily   b. Sofia   c. Emily and Sofia

5. a. Emily   b. Sofia   c. Emily and Sofia

B Look at the pictures in 2A again. Circle the correct answers.

1. Sofia and Emily (was / (were)) students in 1998.

2. Sofia (was / wasn't) a childcare worker in 2003. She (was / wasn't) a server.

3. Emily (was / is) a student in 2011. She (was / was not) a teacher.

4. Sofia (was / wasn't) a childcare worker in 2011. She (was / wasn't) a home health aide.

5. Sofia and Emily (are / were) good friends today.

C Talk to a partner. Follow the directions.

Student A: Make true and false statements about the pictures in 2A.

Student B: Say: *That's true.* or *That's false.* Then correct the false statement.

A: *Sofia and Emily were students in 1998.*   A: *Emily was a gardener in 1998.*

B: *That's true. They were students.*   B: *That's false. She was a student.*

3 Practice: ask and answer *yes/no* questions

A Study the grammar. Listen to the questions and answers. Underline the subject and verb in each question. Notice the word order.

3-25

Yes/No questions and answers	
A: Were you a doctor ten years ago? **B:** Yes, I was. *or* No, I wasn't.	**A:** Were you at home last night? **B:** Yes, we were. *or* No, we weren't.
A: Was he a student five months ago? **B:** Yes, he was. *or* No, he wasn't.	**A:** Were they at school last week? **B:** Yes they were. *or* No, they weren't.

B Work with the grammar. Match the questions with the answers.

1. _____ Were they at school yesterday?
2. _____ Was she a student in 2006?
3. _____ Was he at home last week?
4. _____ Were we late for class this morning?

a. Yes, you were.
b. Yes, he was.
c. No, they weren't.
d. Yes, she was.

C Complete the questions. Then write the answers.

1. _____ Rico a farmer 20 years ago? <u>Yes, he was.</u>
2. _____ Rico a student last year? _____
3. _____ you a student in 2016? _____
4. _____ you at school yesterday? _____

4 Ask and answer questions about the past

A Write a list of your work or school experience in your notebook.

office manager
English student

B Share your list with a partner. Ask and answer questions about the list.

A: Were you a student in 2016?

B: Yes, I was.

A: Were you an office manager in 2016?

B: No, I wasn't. I was an office manager in 2012.

C Work with two classmates. Make a list of all the job experiences in your group.

D Work with your class. Make sentences about the most common jobs in your class.

Four people were cooks. Three people were business owners.

▶▶ TEST YOURSELF

Close your book. Write three sentences about your work experience.

I was a student in 2014. I was a restaurant server in 2016. I'm a receptionist now.

1 Learn about a job interview

🔊
3-26
A Look at Isabel Monte's job application. Listen to the interview.

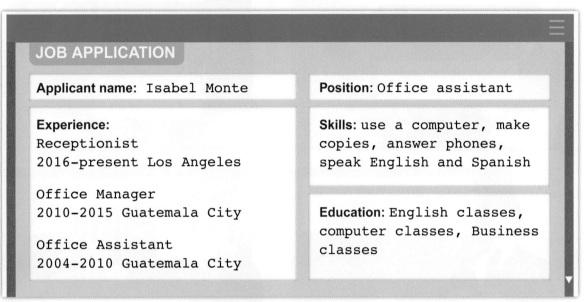

JOB APPLICATION

Applicant name: Isabel Monte

Position: Office assistant

Experience:
Receptionist
2016-present Los Angeles

Office Manager
2010-2015 Guatemala City

Office Assistant
2004-2010 Guatemala City

Skills: use a computer, make copies, answer phones, speak English and Spanish

Education: English classes, computer classes, Business classes

🔊
3-27
B Look at the application in 1A. Listen and write the answers.

1. ___Monte___   4. _____

2. _____   5. _____

3. _____   6. _____

2 Practice your pronunciation

🔊
3-28
A Listen and repeat the sentences. Listen to the stress of *can* and *can't*.

Can	Can't
I can make copies.	I can't drive a bus.
Jose can speak English.	He can't speak Chinese.

🔊
3-29
B Listen for *can* or *can't*. Circle *a* or *b*.

1. a. can (b.) can't   3. a. can   b. can't   5. a. can   b. can't

2. a. can   b. can't   4. a. can   b. can't   6. a. can   b. can't

C Work with a partner. Talk about things you can and can't do. Pay attention to the stress of *can* and *can't*.

I can paint buildings. I can't speak Chinese.

3 Practice answering interview questions

A Listen and read the conversation. Does Mr. Tran get the job?

B Listen and circle *a* or *b*.

1. a. Yes, he is. b. No, he isn't. 4. a. Yes, he can. b. No, he can't.
2. a. Yes, he does. b. No, he doesn't. 5. a. Yes, he can. b. No, he can't.
3. a. Yes, he was. b. No, he wasn't. 6. a. Yes, he can. b. No, he can't.

C Think about the grammar. Find the question and short answer with *can*. What do you notice about the word order?

D Work with a partner. Use the charts to make questions and answers.

Questions with can			Answers					
Can	you he she they	use a computer? drive? take care of children? speak English?	Yes,	I he she they	can.	No,	I he she they	can't.

E Work with a group. Ask and answer *yes/no* questions with *can*. Talk about the people in your group.

A: Marco, can you paint houses? A: Sara, can Marco paint houses?

B: Yes, I can. B: Yes, he can.

4 Make conversation: job interview

A Work with a partner. Make a new conversation.

A: Tell me about yourself, _____ .

B: I'm from _____ . I came here _____ years ago.

A: Do you have work experience?

B: Yes, I do. I worked in a _____ . I was a _____

for _____ years. I can _____ , and _____ .

A: That's great. You're hired!

B Present your conversation to another pair. Observe their conversation.

NEED HELP?

A: Do you have work experience?

B: Yes, I do. *or*
No, I don't, but I can learn quickly.

AT WORK ▸ Job interview skills

🔊 3-32 **A** Listen to the advice for job interviews.

1. Make eye contact.

2. Smile and look friendly.

3. Sit straight. Don't move a lot.

B Work with two partners. Take turns.

Student A: Ask the job interview questions in 4A.

Student B: Answer the questions. Practice your job interview skills.

Student C: Observe Student B. Does he/she make eye contact? Look friendly? Sit straight?

▸▸ TEST YOURSELF

Work with a partner. Tell a partner about three job skills you have. Then change roles.

I can fix sinks. I can speak English and Chinese. I can drive a truck.

1 Build reading strategies

A **Read the definitions. Who does a manager supervise?**

employee: (noun) worker

employer: (noun) person or company that you work for

boss: (noun) the person you work for; your supervisor or manager

co-workers: (noun) people who work with you; other employees

communication: (noun) telling people your ideas and feelings; understanding other people's ideas and feelings

B **Preview the article. Read the title and the headings.**

1. Who is this article for?

☐ employees ☐ employers

2. Do you think this information is for all employees or only for some employees? Why?

C **Read the article.**

Are You Good or Are You Great?

What is a great employee?
We asked some employers, and here are some of their answers:

Great employees are great at communication.

They always read emails and employee information from the boss. When they have a question or a problem, they talk to their co-workers or their supervisors.

Great employees are great co-workers.

They help co-workers and they ask co-workers for advice. They are friendly and calm. They don't get angry a lot.

Great employees want to succeed[1].

They come to work on time or a little early every day. They complete their work on time. They always try to learn more about the job.

[1]succeed: do well

> **READER'S NOTE**
> Writers often use an *example* after an idea. The example helps you understand the idea.

 D **Listen and read the article again. Are you a great employee? Which things do *you* do?**
3-33

E **Complete the sentences. Fill in the bubble next to the correct answer.**

1. According to the article, great employees _____ .
   - ⓐ talk to their bosses
   - ⓑ talk to their co-workers
   - ⓒ a and b

2. According to the article, great employees _____ .
   - ⓐ ask their co-workers for help
   - ⓑ help their customers
   - ⓒ a and b

3. A *calm* person is usually _____ .
   - ⓐ angry
   - ⓑ relaxed
   - ⓒ tired

4. According to the article, great employees _____ .
   - ⓐ don't make mistakes
   - ⓑ come to work on time
   - ⓒ a and b

2 Read about why people lose their jobs

A **Read the chart and complete the sentences below.**

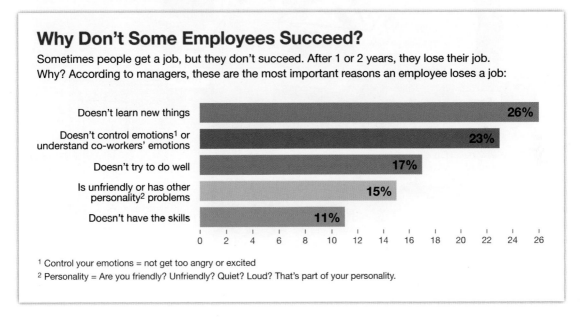

Why Don't Some Employees Succeed?

Sometimes people get a job, but they don't succeed. After 1 or 2 years, they lose their job. Why? According to managers, these are the most important reasons an employee loses a job:

- Doesn't learn new things — 26%
- Doesn't control emotions[1] or understand co-workers' emotions — 23%
- Doesn't try to do well — 17%
- Is unfriendly or has other personality[2] problems — 15%
- Doesn't have the skills — 11%

(scale: 0 2 4 6 8 10 12 14 16 18 20 22 24 26)

[1] Control your emotions = not get too angry or excited
[2] Personality = Are you friendly? Unfriendly? Quiet? Loud? That's part of your personality.

1. _____ percent of the managers say employees lose their jobs because they don't learn new things.

2. _____ percent of the managers say employees lose their jobs because they have personality problems.

B **Work with your class. Look at the chart and article in 2A. Discuss the questions.**

1. Which parts of the chart describe employees who are not good at communication?

2. Which parts of the chart describe employees who don't want to succeed?

 BRING IT TO LIFE

Look at a job ad online. Find 2–3 words that describe the employee they are looking for. Copy the words and share them with your class.

TEAMWORK & LANGUAGE REVIEW

A **Work with a team. Look at the picture. Complete the story.**

1. Rosa is (for / from) Mexico.

2. She (was / were) a teacher in Mexico.

3. She (is / can) teach math and computers.

4. She (can / is) also repair computers.

5. Now she (live / lives) in California.

6. She (is / was) studying English at night and working at a computer company (at / in) the morning.

7. She (repairs / repair) computers. She likes her job, but she (can / wants) to teach.

B **Work with a team. Choose one of the other people in the picture. Write a story about that person. Share your story with the class.**

Her / his name is…   She / he was a … in …   She / he can …

C Interview three classmates. Write their answers in the chart.

	Name: _____	Name: _____	Name: _____
What was your job in your home country?			
Do you have the same job now?	YES NO	YES NO	YES NO
Do you *want* the same job or a different one?	SAME / DIFFERENT	SAME / DIFFERENT	SAME / DIFFERENT

D Discuss your results with the class. How many classmates have the same job? How many want the same job? How many want a different job?

PROBLEM SOLVING

3-34

A Listen and read about Mrs. Galvan. What is the problem?

Mrs. Galvan moved to San Diego this week. She's looking for a job. She can work weekdays, but she can't work on weekends. Mrs. Galvan was a restaurant manager in Los Angeles. She can use a computer, cook, and serve food. Mrs. Galvan is worried. She needs to start work this week.

RESTAURANT JOBS

Food Server
PT, M-F 9-2:00
$8 per hour + tips

Restaurant Manager
Nights and weekends
$24 per hour

Assistant Manager
FT, M-F 8:30 a.m.-4:30 p.m.
$19 per hour

B Work with your classmates. Look at the ads and answer the questions. (More than one answer is possible.)

What is the best job for Mrs. Galvan? Why?

C Work with your classmates. Make a list of other jobs Mrs. Galvan can do.

UNIT

11 Safety First

A LOOK AT
- Safety
- Making suggestions
- Preparing for emergencies

LESSON 1 VOCABULARY

1 Learn about traffic signs and rules

A Show what you know. Circle the words you understand.

1. school crossing	2. road work	3. speed limit	4. no left turn	5. no parking
a. be careful	b. slow down	c. obey	d. turn	e. get a ticket

B Listen and look at the pictures. What is the difference between words 1–5 and words a–e?
3-35

C Listen and repeat the words from 1A.
3-36

D Look at the pictures. Complete the sentences.

1. The ___no left turn___ sign with the black arrow means you can't turn left.
2. There's a yellow _____ sign. You need to be careful and watch for children.
3. Drive 35 miles per hour here. Always obey the _____ .
4. There's an orange _____ sign. Slow down because people are working here.
5. The _____ sign means you can't park here. You don't want to get a ticket.

E Talk to a partner. Ask and answer questions about the pictures in 1A.

A: What color is the road work sign?
B: It's orange.
A: What does it mean?
B: It means people are working. Slow down and be careful.

2 Talk about work safety

A Work in a team. Match the words with the pictures.

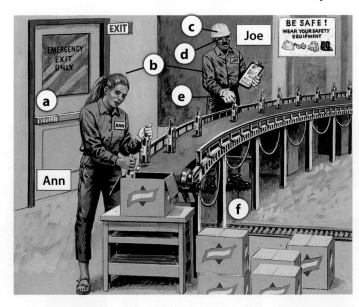

_____ careful   _____ factory workers   _____ safety boots

_____ careless   _____ fire extinguisher   _____ safety glasses

_____ dangerous/unsafe   _____ hard hat   _____ safety gloves

_a_ emergency exit   _____ safe   _____ wet floor

B Listen and check your answers. Then practice the words with a partner.

3-37

C Look at the factory workers. Match the names with the descriptions.

_b_ 1. Ann   a. He's careless. He doesn't see the wet floor.

_____ 2. Joe   b. She's careless. She isn't wearing her safety boots.

_____ 3. Tim   c. She's careful. She wears safety glasses and safety gloves.

_____ 4. Tanya   d. He's careful. He's wearing safety glasses and safety gloves.

D Think about it. Ask and answer the questions with your classmates.

1. What kind of traffic signs do you see on your street?

2. Where can you buy safety equipment?

3. Why is work safety important for employees and employers?

▶▶ **TEST YOURSELF**

Use your notebook. Copy this chart.
Put words from the lesson in the chart.

Traffic signs	Safety equipment	Adjectives

1 Prepare to write

A Talk about the pictures. Is Frank worried?

B Look at the pictures. Listen to the paragraph.

3-38

C Listen again and read about Frank's safety habits.

3-38

I'm not a very careful person. On the road, I always drive fast. I never wear a seat belt. My friends worry, but I don't. At work, I always text my friends. My co-workers say it's not safe, but I don't worry. I never check the smoke detectors at home. My sister worries, but I don't. My sister, my friends, and my co-workers worry too much. They should relax.

Oh, no! Here comes a police officer. Maybe I should worry now.

WRITER'S NOTE
Use *frequency adverbs*, such as *always*, *usually*, *sometimes*, and *never* to show how often you do something. We usually put them between the subject and verb.

D Check your understanding. Circle the correct words.

1. Frank ((drives) / doesn't drive) fast.

2. He (always / never) wears a seat belt.

3. His friends (worry / don't worry).

4. Frank uses his (sofa / cell phone) at work.

5. Frank's sister (worries / doesn't worry) about him.

6. Frank isn't (careful / careless).

E Listen and complete the sentences.

3-39

1. She's usually a very _____ person.

2. She has a _____ detector in her kitchen.

3. She always wears her _____ equipment at work.

4. She _____ in the car.

5. She usually _____ .

2 Plan

A Complete the chart. Check *always*, *usually*, *sometimes*, *never*.

I	always	usually	sometimes	never
wear a seatbelt.				
text or talk on my phone in the car.				
drive fast.				
check my smoke detectors.				

B Work with a partner. Discuss your answers. Add one more item to the chart.

3 Write

A Write a paragraph about your safety habits.

My Safety Habits

I am usually _____ person. I _____ drive

fast. I _____ wear a seat belt. I _____ talk on a

cell phone at work or in a car. I _____ check my smoke detector. I

am _____ careful at work and at home.

B Share your paragraph. Read your paragraph to a partner.

▶▶ TEST YOURSELF

Complete the following sentences. Share your response with your teacher.

1. After this writing lesson, I can…
2. I need more help with…

1 Explore *should* and *should not*: meaning and form

A Look at the poster. Read the sentences. How can people be safe at home?

B Analyze the sentences in 1A. What does *should* mean?

C Study the form. Read the charts.

Should* and *should not					
Statements					
I You He She	should	lock the door.	We You They	should	lock the door.

Negative statements						**Contractions**
I You He She	should not	walk alone.	We You They	should not	walk alone.	should not = shouldn't You shouldn't walk alone.

D Complete the sentences with *should* or *shouldn't*. Use the sentences in 1A.

1. You _____ leave your windows open at night.
2. You _____ walk in the parking lot with other people.
3. You _____ close the building door.
4. You _____ open the door to strangers.

2 Practice: *should* and *shouldn't*

A Listen to the statements about the picture. Circle *True* or *False*.
3-40

1. True   False   3. True   False   5. True   False
2. True   False   4. True   False   6. True   False

B Look at the picture in 2A. Complete the sentences. Use *should* or *shouldn't*.

1. The ladder is broken. They _____ use it.

2. The chemicals are dangerous. They _____ be careful.

3. Gladys or Bill _____ close the door.

4. The fan is broken. They _____ tell the manager.

5. The floor is wet. They _____ walk there.

6. Gladys and Bill _____ wear safety gloves.

C Talk to a partner. Follow the directions.

Student A: Make statements about the picture in 2A.

Student B: Agree or disagree. Tell why.

A: *Gladys should help Karen mop the floor.*

B: *I disagree. She doesn't need help.*

3 Ask and answer information questions with *should*

A Study the grammar. Listen to the questions and answers. Underline all the subjects and verbs. Notice how the questions are different from the answers.

3-41

Information questions and answers with *should*	
A: How often should she check the smoke alarm? **B:** She should check it twice a year.	**A:** What should they do? **B:** They should lock the door.

B Work with the grammar. Match the questions with the answers.

_____ 1. Sara has to walk home at night. What should she do?

_____ 2. I'm lost. I need directions. What should I do?

_____ 3. Bob's windows are open. It's midnight. What should he do?

_____ 4. Frank and I drive too fast. What should we do?

_____ 5. Jen and Fred don't have safety glasses. What should they do?

a. He should close them.

b. She should walk with a friend.

c. They should buy some.

d. You should ask for help.

e. You should slow down.

4 Use *should* to talk about classroom rules

A Work with two classmates. Answer the questions. What should students do in class? What shouldn't they do?

B Complete the chart with the rules of your class.

Follow Classroom Rules! It's Easy!	
Students should...	**Students shouldn't...**
1. _speak English in class_	4. _text in class_
2. _____	5. _____
3. _____	6. _____

C Share your chart with your classmates. Make sentences about the rules.

Students shouldn't text in class.

▶▶ TEST YOURSELF

Close your books. Write three sentences about your school's safety rules. Use *should* or *shouldn't*. Compare your sentences with a partner.

1 Listen to learn: calling 911

A Talk about the pictures with your class. Which words are new to you?

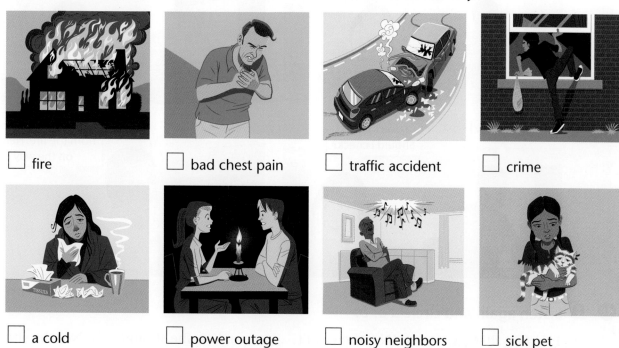

☐ fire   ☐ bad chest pain   ☐ traffic accident   ☐ crime

☐ a cold   ☐ power outage   ☐ noisy neighbors   ☐ sick pet

B Look at the pictures again. When should you call 911? Check (✔) the pictures.

🔊 3-42 **C** Listen and check your answers.

2 Practice your pronunciation

🔊 3-43 **A** Listen for *should* or *shouldn't*. Circle *a* or *b*.

1. a. should
   b. shouldn't

2. a. should
   b. shouldn't

3. a. should
   b. shouldn't

4. a. should
   b. shouldn't

5. a. should
   b. shouldn't

6. a. should
   b. shouldn't

B Work with a partner. Partner A: Read the sentence. Partner B: Respond. Take turns.

1. I have a headache.
2. I can't sleep.
3. There's a fire in the kitchen.
4. I need a prescription.
5. There's a bad car accident.
6. Someone is breaking my neighbor's window.

A: *I have a headache.*

B: *You shouldn't call 911.*

3 Practice calling 911

A Listen and read. What's the emergency?

911. Emergency.

There's a fire at my neighbor's house.

What's the address?

It's 412 Oak Street.

Is anyone hurt?

I don't know. Should I check?

No. Please stay away from the fire. Help is on the way.

B Listen again and circle *a* or *b*.

1. a. Yes, there is.   b. No, there isn't.   3. a. Yes, she should.   b. No, she shouldn't.
2. a. Yes, it is.   b. No, it isn't.   4. a. Yes, it is.   b. No, it isn't.

C Think about the grammar. Look at the conversation. Find the question with *should*. What do you notice about the word order?

D Study the grammar. Listen and repeat.

Yes/No questions with *should*	
Should I call 911? Yes, you should.	Should we lock the doors? Yes, we should.
Should he call the police? No, he shouldn't.	Should they wear safety gloves? Yes. They should.

E Look at these problems. Ask and answer questions with a partner.

toothache

tornado

stolen bicycle

car crash

A: *Should I call 911 for a toothache?*

B: *No, you shouldn't. You should call the dentist.*

4 Make conversation: calling 911

A Talk to a partner. Make a new conversation. Use your own ideas.

A: 911. Emergency.

B: _____ .

A: What's the address?

B: It's _____ .

A: Is anyone hurt?

B: _____ .

A: OK. _____ is on the way.

NEED HELP?

A police officer is on the way.

An ambulance is on the way.

B Present your conversation to another pair. Observe their conversation.

AT WORK > Suggest preparing for an emergency

A Listen and read the conversations.

3-47

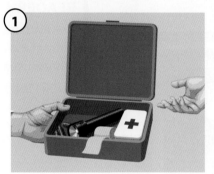

①

A: Should we check the emergency kits? They're getting old.

B: You're right. Can you do that, please?

②

A: Should we plan a fire drill soon?

B: Yes, good idea.

③

A: I think we should have an earthquake drill.

B: Yes, we should.

B Work with a partner. Practice the conversations in A. Then suggest preparing for another emergency.

▶▶ TEST YOURSELF

Close your book. Work with a partner.

Student A: Report an emergency.
Student B: Ask for more information. Tell your partner that help is on the way.
Then change roles.

1 Build reading strategies

A Read the definitions.

pull over: (verb) to drive the car to the side of the road and stop in a safe place

cause: (verb) to make something happen

pay attention: (verb) look, listen, and be careful

pull over

B Preview the article. Read the title and the bold text.

What is the article about?

_____ Things drivers should and shouldn't do

_____ Things drivers like and don't like to do

C Read the article. What is the source of this information?

> ## Be Safe, Be Smart, Pull Over
>
> According to the National Safety Council, unsafe drivers cause millions of car accidents in the U.S. every year. Some of these drivers are going too fast, and some of them are drinking alcohol. However, most of them are just distracted.
>
> **Pay Attention**
>
> What is distracted driving?
>
> 1. **Not looking at the road** Are you looking at your phone? At your friend in the car? At a nearby traffic accident? Then you are distracted!
>
> 2. **Taking your hands off the steering wheel** Are you eating? Drinking coffee? Brushing your hair? Then you are distracted!
>
> 3. **Not thinking about driving** Are you having an interesting conversation? Are you listening to your music? Then you are distracted!
>
> Distracted driving is dangerous driving. Be a safe driver. Pay attention to the road or pull over.

READER'S NOTE

However means the same thing as *but*. Writers usually use it at the beginning of a sentence.

 D Listen and read the article again.

3-48

E Read the questions. Fill in the bubble next to the correct answer.

1. You should _____ when you drive a car.
   (a) pay attention
   (b) pull over
   (c) a and b

2. *Distracted* means _____ .
   (a) not obeying the speed limit
   (b) not paying attention
   (c) going too fast

3. Texting when driving is bad because _____ .
   (a) you're not looking at the road
   (b) you don't have your hands on the wheel
   (c) a and b

4. If you are distracted, you should _____ .
   (a) call the police
   (b) pull over
   (c) a and b

2 Read about distracted driving and teenagers

A Look at the poster and complete the sentences.

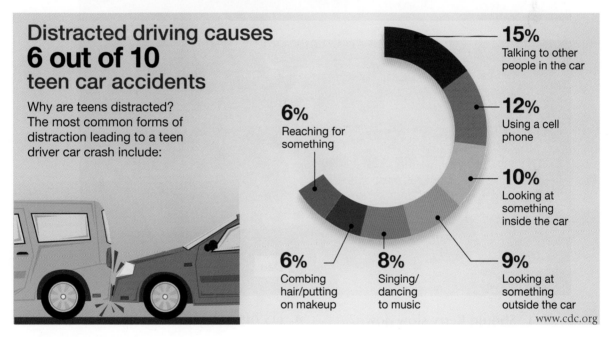

Distracted driving causes
6 out of 10
teen car accidents

Why are teens distracted? The most common forms of distraction leading to a teen driver car crash include:

6% Reaching for something

6% Combing hair/putting on makeup

8% Singing/ dancing to music

9% Looking at something outside the car

10% Looking at something inside the car

12% Using a cell phone

15% Talking to other people in the car

www.cdc.org

1. For every 10 teen car accidents, distracted driving causes _____ of them.

2. Twelve percent of teens are distracted because they are _____ .

B Think about it. Discuss the questions with your classmates.

1. Look at the kinds of distracted driving in the chart. Which ones are examples of not looking at the road? Which are examples of taking your hands off the steering wheel?

2. Do you do some of these things? Which ones? How often?

3. Why don't people pull over when they should?

 BRING IT TO LIFE

Search for "distracted driving" in the news section of a search engine. Choose one headline to copy. Look up the words you don't know. Share the headline with your class.

TEAMWORK & LANGUAGE REVIEW

A Work with a team. Look at the pictures. Match the questions and answers.

_____ 1. Should Kerry slow down?
_____ 2. Should Tim call 911?
_____ 3. What should Kerry do?
_____ 4. What should Dan do?
_____ 5. Who should call 911?

a. Fix his smoke alarm.
b. Dan.
c. Pull over.
d. Yes, she should.
e. No, he shouldn't.

B Work with a team. What should the people in the pictures do? What shouldn't they do? Write as many sentences as you can.

C Share your sentences with a classmate from another team.

D Work with your class. Write a paragraph about the people in the pictures.

Kerry, Tim, and Dan are very careless people. Kerry always drives very fast. She…

E Interview three classmates. Ask the question. Write their answers in the chart.
Everyone is careless sometimes. How should you be more careful?

Name	should/shouldn't...

F Work with a partner. Make a chart to categorize the ways your classmates should be more careful.

at home	in the car	at work or school	outside

G Report your results to the class. Summarize the class results.

Six of us should be more careful at home.

PROBLEM SOLVING

A Listen and read about Mr. Brown. What is the problem?

3-49

Mr. Brown is in the parking lot at the supermarket. He's very tired. He's parking his car and he doesn't see the car next to him! He hits it. It's a small accident. He looks around the parking lot, but the driver of the other car is not there.

B Work with your classmates. Answer the question: What should Mr. Brown do? (More than one answer is possible.)

a. Call 911.　　　c. Talk to the market manager.

b. Stay there.　　d. Other: _____

C Write a note that Mr. Brown can leave for the other driver.

	To Whom It May Concern:
	I'm sorry I hit your car. It was an _____.
	Please _____ at (304) 555-3167.
	Sincerely,

UNIT

12 What's Next?

A LOOK AT
- Leisure
- Future with *be going to*
- Encouraging others

LESSON **1** VOCABULARY

1 Learn weather words and holidays

A Show what you know. Circle the words you use.

1. snowing   2. raining   3. cloudy   4. sunny   5. hot   6. cold

B Listen and look at the pictures. When is Father's Day? How's the weather?

3-50

C Listen and repeat the words from 1A.

3-51

D Write the vocabulary. Look at the pictures. Complete the sentences.

1. It's _____ this Independence Day.
2. It's _____ this Thanksgiving.
3. It's _____ this Father's Day.
4. It's _____ this New Year's Day.
5. It's _____ this Mother's Day.
6. It's _____ this Presidents' Day.

E Talk to a partner. Ask and answer questions. Use the pictures in 1A.

A: How's the weather in July in _____ ?
B: It's hot.

2 Talk about leisure activities

A Work in a team. Match the words with the pictures.

winter

spring

summer

fall

_____ go out to eat	_____ go to the movies	_____ play soccer
_____ go swimming	_____ have a picnic	_a_ stay home
_____ go to the beach	_____ make a snowman	

B Listen and check your answers. Then practice the words with a partner.

3-52

C Look at the pictures. Circle the correct words.

1. In the winter, it's (cold / hot). The Kotas like to (play soccer / stay home).
2. The flowers are beautiful in the (fall / spring). They like to have (movies / picnics).
3. The weather is (hot / cold) in the summer. They like to (go / stay) to the beach.
4. In the fall, they like to go (out to eat / to the beach). Other people like to go (swimming / to the movies).

D Think about it. Ask and answer the questions with your classmates.

1. What is your favorite time of the year? Why?
2. What is your favorite holiday? Why?

E Copy the new words in your vocabulary notebook.

▶▶ **TEST YOURSELF**

Use your notebook. Copy this chart.
Put words from the lesson in the chart.

Holidays	Weather	Activities

1 Prepare to write

A Talk about the picture. What does the man want to do on his day off?

B Look at the picture. Listen to the story.

3-53

C Listen again and read the paragraph.

3-53

Ready for Time Off

I work at the post office five days a week. Saturday and Sunday are my days off. On Saturdays I study because I'm applying for a promotion at work. But on Sundays I have fun with my son. This Sunday, we're going to see a baseball game. We're going to watch the game and eat hot dogs. My son wants to catch a ball at the game. I can't wait for the weekend!

WRITER'S NOTE
Paragraphs sometimes end with a *concluding* sentence. This sentence tells an important idea from the paragraph.

D Check your understanding. Circle *a* or *b*.

1. Saturday and Sunday are his _____ .
   a. work days   b. days off

2. He wants _____ .
   a. a new job   b. a promotion

3. They're going to see a baseball game _____ .
   a. on Saturday   b. on Sunday

4. He's going to see the game with his _____ .
   a. boss   b. son

5. His son wants to catch a _____ at the game.
   a. ball   b. hot dog

6. They're going to _____ hot dogs.
   a. see   b. eat

E **Listen and complete the sentences.**
3-54

1. She works _____ .

2. She goes to school _____ .

3. Monday is _____ .

4. She usually _____ .

5. This Monday, she's going to _____ .

 F **Compare sentences with your partner. Listen again and check your work.**
3-54

2 Plan

A **Get ready to write. Talk about the questions with your classmates.**

1. When do you go to school or work?

2. What are your days off?

3. What do you do on your days off?

4. What are you going to do on your next day off?

3 Write

A **Write a paragraph.**

> **Ready for Time Off**
>
> by _____
>
> I _____ . I don't _____
>
> on _____ . This _____ ,
>
> I'm going to _____ . I can't wait for
>
> _____ !

B **Edit your paragraph. Check your punctuation and your concluding sentence. Then read your paragraph to a partner.**

▶▶ **TEST YOURSELF**

Complete the following sentences. Share your response with your teacher.

1. After this writing lesson, I can…
2. I need more help with…

1 Explore the future with *be going to*: form and meaning

A Look at the pictures. Which plans are for fun? Which plans are for her career?

On Saturday I'm going to have a picnic.

This fall I'm going to take a computer class.

In two years I'm going to be a computer technician.

B Analyze the sentences in 1A. Underline the future verbs. How many parts does each verb have?

C Study the form. Read the charts.

The future with *be going to*

Statements

I	am			We			
You	are	going to	play soccer.	You			
He She	is				are	going to	play soccer.
It	is	going to	be sunny.	They			

Negative statements

I	am			We			
You	are	not going to	play soccer.	You			
He She	is				are	not going to	play soccer.
It	is	not going to	be sunny.	They			

D Work with a partner. Say the sentences in the charts.

2 Practice: the future with *be going to*

3-55 **A** Listen to the statements. Look at the picture. Circle the correct answer.

1. a. Mel
   b. Maya
   c. both a and b

2. a. Kima
   b. Gina
   c. Lee

3. a. Mel
   b. Gina and Kala
   c. both a and b

4. a. Lee and Pam
   b. Mel and Maya
   c. Kima

B Look at the picture in 2A. Circle the correct words.

1. It's a beautiful day. It's going to (were / be) sunny all weekend.
2. Kima is (going to / going) go to the pool with her children.
3. Mel and Maya (is / are) going to exercise at the gym.
4. The children (are go to / are going to) play in the park.
5. Lee and Pam (were / was) at the theater.
6. They're going to (eating / eat) lunch soon.

C Talk to a partner. Follow the directions. Then change roles.

Student A: Make statements about the picture in 2A.

Student B: Name the person or people you hear about.

A: *He's going to go to the gym.*

B: *That's Mel.*

3 Ask and answer questions with *be going to*

A Study the grammar. Listen to the questions and answers. Underline the complete verb in each one. Notice how many parts it has.

3-56

Information questions with *be going to*	
A: What are you going to do tonight? **B:** I'm going to study.	**A:** What are we going to do next week? **B:** We're going to (go to) Mexico.
A: What is he going to do tomorrow? **B:** He's going to see a movie.	**A:** What are they going to do next year? **B:** They're going to take a computer class.

B Work with the grammar. Write the questions.

1. <u>What is she going to do tonight</u> ? She's going to watch TV tonight.
2. _____ ? I'm going to have a picnic on Saturday.
3. _____ ? We're going to have fun this weekend.
4. _____ ? They're going to study tomorrow.
5. _____ ? He's going to apply for a promotion next year.

4 Talk about future plans with your classmates

A Complete the questions. Use the words in the box. Then write your answers.

What	Who	When	Where

1. <u>Where</u> are you going to go after class? _____<u>I'm going to go home.</u>_____
2. _____ are you going to do tomorrow? _____
3 _____ are you going to see a movie? _____
4. _____ are you going to talk to after class? _____

B Ask and answer the questions in 4A with a partner. Then write sentences about your partner's plans.

Juan is going to go to work after class.

▶▶ TEST YOURSELF

Close your book. Write a sentence about your weekend plans. Write two sentences about your plans for next year.

I'm going to play soccer in the park on Saturday.
Next summer I'm going to take a vacation.
Next winter I'm going to get a new job.

1 Learn about making plans

A Look at the catalog with your classmates. Which words are new to you?

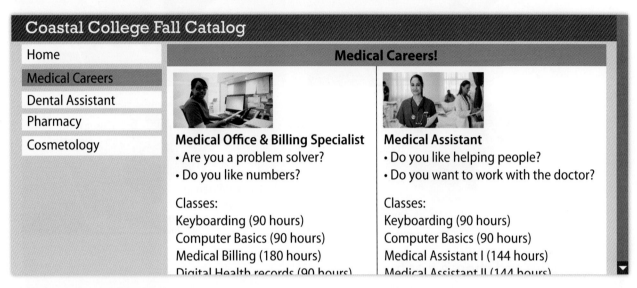

B Look at the catalog page and check (✔) the answers in the chart.

	medical billing specialist	medical assistant	both
works with numbers			
works with the doctor			
knows keyboarding			
knows computer basics			

C Listen to the ad for Coastal Community College. Which classes are a good start for most careers? Do you agree with the ad? Why or why not?

3-57

2 Practice your pronunciation

A Listen to the sentences. What is different in the relaxed pronunciation?

3-58

Formal	Relaxed
A: What are we going to do today? **B:** We're going to go to the park.	**A:** What are we going to do today? **B:** We're going to go to the park.

B Work with a partner. Read the questions and answers in 3A on page 164. Practice formal and relaxed pronunciation.

3 Discuss plan and goals

A Listen and read the conversation.

3-59

B Listen and choose *a* or *b*.

3-60

1. a. Yes, she is.
   b. No, she isn't.

2. a. Yes, she was.
   b. No, she wasn't.

3. a. Yes, she does.
   b. No, she doesn't.

4. a. Yes, it does.
   b. No, it doesn't.

C Think about the grammar. Look at the conversation again and answer the questions.

1. Which question is about the past?
2. Which questions are about the future?

D Work with a partner. Use the charts to make new questions and answers.

Questions with *be*								
Present			**Future**			**Past**		
Are they	at home?	Yes, they are.	Are they going to be	at home?	Yes, they are.	Were they	at home?	Yes, they were.
	at work?	No, they aren't.		at work?	No, they aren't.		at work?	No, they weren't.

E Work with a partner. Say the questions and answers in the chart with *he* or *she*. What happens to the verbs?

4 Make conversation

A Work with a partner. Make a new conversation.

A: What are your plans for _____ ?

B: I'm going to _____ .

A: That's great! When _____ ?

B: _____ . How about you? What are your plans?

A: I'm going to _____ .

A: That's great!

NEED HELP?

What are your plans for…
next weekend?
the summer?
the future?

B Present your conversation to another pair. Observe their conversation.

AT WORK ▷ Encouraging others

A Listen and read the conversations.

3-61

B Work with a partner. Practice the conversations in A. Then tell a partner about something you want to do. Take turns encouraging each other.

▶▶ TEST YOURSELF

Talk to three people. Tell them your plans for next weekend and next year. Listen to their plans and encourage them.

1 Build reading strategies

A Read the definitions.

goal: (noun) something you want to do

job counselor: (noun) a person who helps you find a job or choose a career

school counselor: (noun) a person who helps you choose classes and study programs

B Preview the article. Read the title and the first paragraph. What is the purpose of this article?

_____ to give information about careers

_____ to tell a funny story

_____ to give advice

> **READER'S NOTE**
>
> An article can have many different *purposes,* such as:
> - give information
> - give advice
> - tell an interesting or funny story

C Read about planning your future. Do you do any of these things when you make plans?

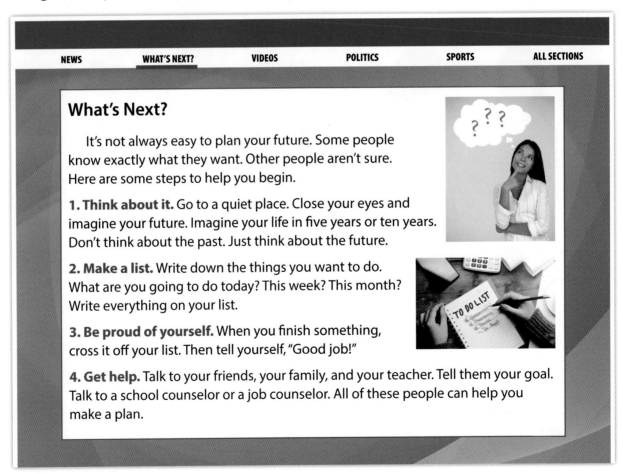

| NEWS | WHAT'S NEXT? | VIDEOS | POLITICS | SPORTS | ALL SECTIONS |

What's Next?

It's not always easy to plan your future. Some people know exactly what they want. Other people aren't sure. Here are some steps to help you begin.

1. Think about it. Go to a quiet place. Close your eyes and imagine your future. Imagine your life in five years or ten years. Don't think about the past. Just think about the future.

2. Make a list. Write down the things you want to do. What are you going to do today? This week? This month? Write everything on your list.

3. Be proud of yourself. When you finish something, cross it off your list. Then tell yourself, "Good job!"

4. Get help. Talk to your friends, your family, and your teacher. Tell them your goal. Talk to a school counselor or a job counselor. All of these people can help you make a plan.

 D Listen and read the article in 1C again.

3-62

E **Complete the sentences. Fill in the bubble next to the correct answer.**

1. *Imagine* means
   - ⓐ think about
   - ⓑ talk about
   - ⓒ laugh about

2. According to the article, you should ____ .
   - ⓐ think about the past
   - ⓑ make a list
   - ⓒ a and b

3. When you finish something, you should ____ .
   - ⓐ write it down
   - ⓑ feel proud
   - ⓒ talk to a counselor

3. ____ can help you make a plan.
   - ⓐ Your friends
   - ⓑ Counselors
   - ⓒ a and b

2 Read about making plans

A **Read Adnan's flowchart. Answer the questions.**

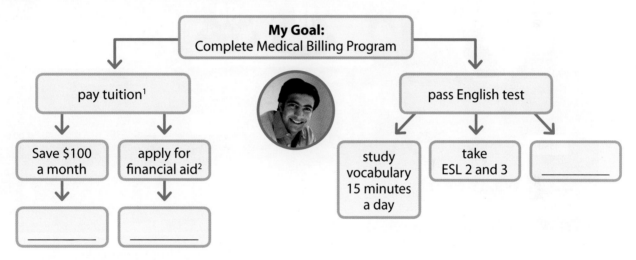

My Goal:
Complete Medical Billing Program

pay tuition¹ → Save $100 a month → _____
pay tuition¹ → apply for financial aid² → _____

pass English test → study vocabulary 15 minutes a day
pass English test → take ESL 2 and 3
pass English test → _____

¹**tuition** = money for school

²**financial aid** = a program to help people pay for college

B **Work with a partner. Look at the flowchart. Answer the questions.**

1. What is Adnan's goal?
2. Which things on the flowchart does he need to do first?

C **Work with a partner. Adnan wants to add these ideas to the flowchart. Where should he put them?**

Make an appointment with a financial aid counselor

Watch the news in English every night

Ask for four more hours a week at work.

 BRING IT TO LIFE

Make a flowchart like Adnan's. Write your goal at the top. Share it with your classmates. Help your classmates add ideas to their flowcharts.

TEAMWORK & LANGUAGE REVIEW

A Work with a team. Look at the picture. Complete the story.

_____ 1. How's the weather?

_____ 2. Why are they having a party?

_____ 3. Who is Gani?

_____ 4. What are they doing now?

_____ 5. What are they going to do next?

a. They're going to eat cake.

b. It's Lou and Gani's birthday.

c. Lou's grandfather.

d. It's warm and sunny.

e. They're singing "Happy Birthday."

B Work with a team. Write 5–7 new questions about the picture.

What...?   Where...?   Why...?   How...?   Who...?   Is...?

C Talk to people from other teams. Ask your questions.

D Work with your class. Write a paragraph about the picture.

Today is Lou and Gani's birthday. ...

E Interview three classmates. Write their answers in the chart.

	Name: _____	Name: _____	Name: _____
What are you going to do on your next day off?			
...next year?			
...in five years?			

F Work with a team. Share your interview data and answer the questions.

1. How many interviewees have fun plans for their day off?

2. How many interviewees are going to continue their education?

3. How may interviewees' lives are going to change a lot in five years?

G Report your results to the class. Summarize the class results.

Twenty-two of us have fun plans for our next day off.

PROBLEM SOLVING

A Listen and read about Linda. What is the problem?

3-63

Linda lives in Chicago. Every year she drives two hours to her brother's house on Thanksgiving Day. Tomorrow is Thanksgiving. Linda is cooking and listening to the radio. The radio says that it's going to snow all night tonight and all day tomorrow. Linda doesn't like to drive in bad weather.

Snow

B Work with your classmates. Answer the question: What can Linda do?

a. Drive to her brother's house now.

b. Take the bus to her brother's house.

c. Have a video chat with her family.

d. Other: _____

Simple present with *be*

Statements		
I	am	
You	are	a student.
He She	is	
It	is	a book.
We You They	are	students.

Negative statements		
I	am not	
You	are not	a student.
He She	is not	
It	is not	a book.
We You They	are not	students.

Contractions	
I am = I'm	I am not = I'm not
you are = you're	you are not = you aren't
he is = he's	he is not = he isn't
she is = she's	she is not = she isn't
it is = it's	it is not = it isn't
we are = we're	we are not = we aren't
they are = they're	they are not = they aren't

Yes/no questions		
Am	I	
Are	you	
Is	he she it	happy?
Are	we you they	

Answers						
	I	am.		I	am not.	
	you	are.		you	aren't.	
Yes,	he she it	is.	No,	he she it	isn't.	
	we you they	are.		we you they	aren't.	

Information questions		
Where	am	I?
How	are	you?
Who	is	he? she?
When	is	it?
Where What	are	we? you? they?

Present continuous

Statements		
I	am	
You	are	
He She It	is	sleeping.
We You They	are	

Negative statements		
I	am not	
You	aren't	
He She It	isn't	sleeping.
We You They	aren't	

Yes/no questions		
Am	I	
Are	you	
Is	he she it	eating?
Are	we you they	

Answers						
	I	am.		I	am not.	
	you	are.		you	aren't.	
Yes,	he she it	is.	No,	he she it	isn't.	
	we you they	are.		we you they	aren't.	

Information questions			
Where	am	I	going?
When	are	you	
Who Why	is	he she	calling?
How	is	it	doing?
What	are	we you they	doing?

Simple present

Statements	
I You	work.
He She It	works.
We You They	work.

Negative statements		
I You	don't	
He She It	doesn't	work.
We You They	don't	

Contractions
do not = don't does not = doesn't

Yes/no questions		
Do	I you	
Does	he she it	work?
Do	we you they	

Answers					
	I you	do.		I you	don't.
Yes,	he she it	does.	No,	he she it	doesn't.
	we you they	do.		we you they	don't.

Information questions			
What	do	I you	study?
Who	does	he she	see?
How	does	it	work?
Where When Why	do	we you they	work?

Simple past with *be*

Statements		
I	was	
You	were	
He She It	was	here.
We You They	were	

Negative statements		
I	wasn't	
You	weren't	
He She It	wasn't	here.
We You They	weren't	

Contractions
was not = wasn't were not = weren't

Yes/no questions		
Was	I	
Were	you	
Was	he she it	late?
Were	we you they	

Answers					
	I	was.		I	wasn't.
	you	were.		you	weren't.
Yes,	he she it	was.	No,	he she it	wasn't.
	we you they	were.		we you they	weren't.

Information questions			
Where	was	I	yesterday?
Why	were	you	in Texas?
Who	was	he? she?	
When	was	it	here?
How What	were	we you they	last year?

Future with *be going to*

Statements

I	am		
You	are	going to	have a party tomorrow.
He She	is		
It	is	going to	rain in two days.
We You They	are	going to	visit friends next week.

Negative statements

I	am not		
You	aren't	going to	have a party tomorrow.
He She	isn't		
It	isn't	going to	rain in two days.
We You They	aren't	going to	visit friends next week.

Yes/no questions

Am	I		
Are	you	going to	have a party?
Is	he she		
Is	it	going to	rain?
Are	we you they	going to	visit friends?

Answers

Yes,	I	am.	No,	I	am not.
	you	are.		you	aren't.
	he she it	is.		he she it	isn't.
	we you they	are.		we you they	aren't.

Information questions

Who	am	I	going to	see?
	are	you		
When What	is	he she it	going to	eat?
How Why What	were	we you they	going to	study?

Can and *should*

Statements

I You He She It We You They	can should	work.

Negative statements

I You He She It We You They	can't shouldn't	work.

Contractions

cannot = can't
should not = shouldn't

Yes/no questions

Can Should	I you he she it we you they	work?

Answers

Yes,	I you he she it we you they	can. should.	No,	I you he she it we you they	can't. shouldn't.

Information questions

Who What	can should	I you	see?
When Why How	can should	he she it	help?
Where	can should	we you they	travel?

There is/there are

Statements

There	is	a pencil.
	are	pencils.

Negative statements

There	isn't	a pencil.
	aren't	pencils.

Yes/no questions

Is	there	a pencil?
Are		pens?

Answers

Yes,	there	is.	No,	there	isn't.
		are.			aren't.

Questions with *how many*

How many	pens	are	there?

Answers

There	is	one pen.
	are	two pens.

This, *that*, *these*, and *those*

Singular statements			
This That	sofa is new.	Use *this* and *these* when the people or things are near.
This That	is new.	

Plural statements			
These Those	sofas are new.	Use *that* and *those* when the people or things are far.
These Those	are new.	

Yes/no questions
Is that sofa new?

Answers
Yes, it is.
No, it isn't.

Yes/no questions
Are these sofas new?

Answers
Yes, they are.
No, they aren't.

A, *an*, *any*, and *some*

Singular questions	
Do you have	a tomato? an onion?

Answers
Yes, I have an onion.
No, I don't have an onion.

Plural questions		
Do you have	any	tomatoes? onions?

Answers
Yes, I have some tomatoes.
No, I don't have any tomatoes.

Nouns

To make plural nouns	Examples	
For most nouns, add -*s*.	chair—chairs	office—offices
If nouns end in -*s*, -*z*, -*sh*, -*ch*, -*x*, add -*es*.	bus—buses	lunch—lunches
If nouns end in consonant + -*y*, change -*y* to -*ies*.	family—families	factory—factories
If nouns end in vowel + -*y*, keep -*y*.	boy—boys	day—days
For most nouns that end in -*o*, add -*s*.	photo—photos	radio—radios
For some nouns that end in -*o*, add -*es*.	tomato—tomatoes	potatoes—potatoes
For most nouns that end in -*f* or -*fe*, change -*f* or -*fe* to *v*. Add -*es*.	wife—wives	half—halves
Some plural nouns do not end in -*s*, -*es*, or -*ies*. They are irregular plurals.	child—children	person—people

Pronouns and possessive adjectives

Subject pronouns
I
you
he
she
it
we
you
they

Object pronouns
me
you
him
her
it
us
you
them

Possessive adjectives
my
your
his
her
its
our
your
their

Possessives

Singular nouns		
Tom's The manager's The factory's The woman's The person's	office is big.	Use -'s after a name, person, or thing for the possessive. Tom's the factory's

Plural regular nouns		
The managers' The factories'	office is big.	For plural nouns, change -s to -s'. the managers'

Plural irregular nouns		
The women's The people's	office is big.	For irregular plurals, add -'s. women's

Information questions		
What color is	my your Tom's Sara's the cat's our your their	hair?

Answers	
My Your His Her Its Our Your Their	hair is black.

Prepositions

Times and dates		
I work	on Tuesday. on June 16th.	Use *on* for days and dates.
The party is	at 9:30. at 9 o'clock.	Use *at* for times.

Locations		
The bank is	next to behind in front of across from	the library.
The bank is	between	the library and the store.

Frequency and time expressions

Frequency expressions			
I You	exercise		
He She It	exercises	every once a twice a three times a	day. week. month. year.
We You They	exercise		

Adverbs of frequency		
I You		exercise.
He She It	always usually sometimes never	exercises.
We You They		exercise.

Questions and answers with *how often*	
A: How often do they exercise? **B:** They exercise every month.	**A:** How often does she exercise? **B:** She usually exercises.
A: How often does he exercise? **B:** He exercises once a day.	**A:** How often do you exercise? **B:** I never exercise.

Statements with *and, but, or*

Note	Examples
To combine sentences, use *and*. Change the first period to a comma.	I need a quarter. Amy wants a dime. I need a quarter, **and** Amy wants a dime.
For sentences with different ideas, use *but*. Change the first period to a comma.	I have a nickel. I don't have a quarter. I have a nickel, **but** I don't have a quarter.
To combine two options, use *or*. Change the first period to a comma.	I want 10¢. I need a dime. I need ten pennies. I want 10¢. I need a dime, **or** I need ten pennies.

OXFORD
UNIVERSITY PRESS

198 Madison Avenue
New York, NY 10016 USA

Great Clarendon Street, Oxford, OX2 6DP, United Kingdom

Oxford University Press is a department of the University of Oxford.
It furthers the University's objective of excellence in research, scholarship,
and education by publishing worldwide. Oxford is a registered trade
mark of Oxford University Press in the UK and in certain other countries

© Oxford University Press 2017

The moral rights of the author have been asserted

First published in 2017

2021 2020 2019

10 9 8 7 6 5 4 3

ISBN: 978 0 19 449269 0 STUDENT BOOK (PACK)

ISBN: 9 78 0 19 449301 7 STUDENT BOOK (PACK COMPONENT)

ISBN: 9 78 0 19 449272 0 ONLINE PRACTICE (PACK COMPONENT)

ISBN: 9 78 0 19 440479 2 OEVT APP

Printed in China

This book is printed on paper from certified and well-managed sources

ACKNOWLEDGMENTS

Back cover photograph: Oxford University Press building/David Fisher

Illustrations by: Cover, Jeff Mangiat / Mendola Artist Representatives; 5W
Infographics, p. 28, p. 29, p. 39, p. 57, p. 68 (bottom), p. 98, p. 106 (bottom), p.
113, p. 132, p. 141, p. 148, p. 155; Silke Bachmann, p.6, p.81 (supermarket);
Ken Batelman, p.61, p.64, p.127, p.148; John Batten, p. 56 (top), p.120; Annie
Bissett, p.28 (map bottom), p.67, p.85 (spot illos); Dan Brown, p.5, p.117;
Gary Bullock, p. 2, p. 24, p. 40, p. 82, p. 92 (bottom), p. 153; Gary Ciccarelli,
p.2 (bottom); Sam and Amy Collins, p.116; Laurie Conley, p.131, p. 163; Phil
Constantinesco, p. 54, p. 138; Mark Duffin, p. 112 (top); Jeff Fillbach, p.14;
Debby Fisher, p.4, p.18; Mike Gardner, p. 4, p. 20, p. 32 (people revision), p.
33, p. 36, p. 59, p. 62, p. 63, p. 67, p. 71, p. 75, p. 85 (chart), p. 89, p. 92 (top),
p. 95, p. 102, p. 103, p. 110 (bottom), p. 117; Martha Gavin, p.34, p. 35, p.62,
p.76, p.90, p.104; John Goodwin, p. 10, p. 13, p. 41, p. 69, p. 97, p. 144, p. 152
(bottom), p. 166; Paul Hampson, p.36, p.92; Mark Hannon, p. 9, p.20, p.118,
p.134, p. 146, p.160; Peter Hoey, p. 53, p. 109; Rod Hunt, p.46, p.47; Janos
Jantner/Beehive Illustration, p. 23, p. 37, p. 72, p. 135, p. 142, p. 156; Ken
Joudrey/Munro Campagna, p. 79; Jon Keegan, p.89, p.126; Uldis Klavins, p.145,
p.149; John Kurtz, p. 26, p. 68 (top), p. 74, p. 96, p. 124, p. 152 (top), p. 167;
Shelton Leong, p. 48, p.70 (top), p.84 (people), p.162; Jeffrey Lindberg, p. 130;
Deb Lofaso, p. 14, p. 42, p. 43, p. 56 (bottom), p. 70, p. 84, p. 112 (bottom), p.
126, p. 137, p. 140, p. 143 (bottom), p. 154, p. 165, p. 168, p. 169; Dan Long, p.
65; Scott MacNeill, p.8, p.62 (locations), p.70 (emergency kit and exit graphic
in realia), p.95 (realia), p.154 (car); Jeff Mangiat/Mendola Art, p. 58; Kevin

McCain, p.150; Derek Mueller, p.103; Karen Minot, p. 100, p.109 (checks);
Tom Newsom, p.75, p.102; Daniel O'Leary/Illustration Ltd., p. 49, p. 51; Terry
Paczko, p.81 (office actions), p. 88; Geo Parkin, p. 30, p. 51, p. 83, p. 106 (top),
p. 121, p. 125, p. 151, p.158; Roger Penwill, p.17, p.31, p.59, p.73, p.87, p.101,
p.115, p.129, p.157, p.171; Karen Prichett, p.32 (original people), p.33; Aaron
Sacco, p. xiii, p. 12, p. 55, p. 78, p. 110 (top), p. 139; Martin Sanders, p. 60, p.
143 (middle); Wendy Wassink, p. 128; Simon Williams/Illustration Ltd., p. 16,
p. 44, p. 86, 114, 170.

*We would also like to thank the following for permission to reproduce the following
photographs*: Click Bestsellers / Shutterstock.com, Cover; Diamond
Photography/Alamy Stock Photo, p. 3 (iPhone); Rafael Croonen/Shutterstock.
com, p. 3 (house number); aldomurillo/Getty Images, p. 6 (young man);
leungchopan/Shutterstock.com, p. 13 (businesswomen and man); sjenner13/
Getty Images, p. 13 (female colleagues); VectorLifestylepic/Shutterstock.com,
p. 14 (female student); michaeljung/Shutterstock.com, p. 14 (male student);
Golden Productions/age fotostock, p. 14 (women talking); wavebreakmedia/
Shutterstock.com, p. 14 (student asking question); SolStock/Getty Images, p.
15 (students & teacher); michaeljung/Shutterstock.com, p. 15 (construction
worker); Monkey Business Images/Shutterstock.com, p. 15 (men talking);
Leonard Zhukovsky/Shutterstock.com, p. 15 (American flag); Susan Vogel/
Getty Images, p. 15 (doctor); 06photo/Shutterstock.com, p. 15 (woman
shopping); Monkey Business Images/Shutterstock.com, p. 15 (student &
teacher); Hongqi Zhang/Alamy Stock Photo, p. 15 (graduate); XiXinXing/
Getty Images, p. 20 (man); Image Source/Alamy Stock Photo, p. 20 (woman);
Ken Weingart/Alamy Stock Photo, p. 22 (man); KidStock/Getty Images, p.
22 (mother & daughter); GK Hart/Vikki Hart/Getty Images, p. 22 (dog); India
Picture/Shutterstock.com, p. 22 (family at graduation); Hayk_Shalunts/
Shutterstock.com, p. 22 (man driving); Stockbyte/Getty Images, p. 22 (tired
businessman); Jessica Peterson/Getty Images, p. 25 (woman); michaeljung/
Shutterstock.com, p. 25 (man); Aflo Relax/Masterfile, p. 25 (bride & groom);
JohnnyGreig/Getty Images, p. 27 (businesswomen); Tetra Images/Getty
Images, p. 27 (man at work); Erik Isakson/Getty Images, p. 42 (adult children);
pixelheadphoto digitalskillet/Getty Images, p. 42 (young children); Design Pics
Inc/Alamy Stock Photo, p. 42 (large family); Oksana Shufrych/Shutterstock.
com, p. 42 (small family); Purestock/Getty Images, p. 45 (man); Mark de Leeuw
Tetra Images/Newscom, p. 50 (woman cleaning); Andrey_Popov/Shutterstock.
com, p. 50 (man cleaning); asiseeit/Getty Images, p. 50 (girls eating lunch);
Antonio Guillem/Shutterstock.com, p. 50 (writing letter); Justin Kase z12z/
Alamy Stock Photo, p. 50 (workers); MaxyM/Shutterstock.com, p. 50 (cat);
XiXinXing/Shutterstock.com, p. 77 (supermarket worker); Jose Luis Pelaez
Inc/Getty Images, p. 83 (doctor & nurse); DreamPictures/Getty Images, p.
83 (coworkers); Tetra Images/Alamy Stock Photo, p. 83 (coworkers at copy
machine); Jetta Productions/Getty Images, p. 83 (construction workers);
Hiya Images/Corbis/Getty Images, p. 83 (bank workers); sturti/Getty Images,
p. 83 (warehouse workers); Minerva Studio/Shutterstock.com, p. 105 (man
shopping); andresr/Getty Images, p. 107 (female supermarket worker);
JeffG/Alamy Stock Photo, p. 107 (male supermarket worker); Vgstockstudio/
Shutterstock.com, p. 111 (pizza delivery person); Monkey Business Images/
Shutterstock.com, p. 111 (customer service worker); XiXinXing/Shutterstock.
com, p. 111 (grocery clerk); Bryan Solomon/Shutterstock.com, p. 119 (donut);
Serg64/Shutterstock.com, p. 119 (apple); Goran Bogicevic/Shutterstock.com,
p. 119 (woman drinking tea); Olena Zaskochenko/Shutterstock.com, p. 123
(woman with fever); Andrey_Popov/Shutterstock.com, p. 123 (sick man);
Apollofoto/Shutterstock.com, p. 123 (man with nasal congestion); deeepblue/
Shutterstock.com, p. 123 (man with sore throat); mm88/Alamy Stock Photo,
p. 123 (woman with cough); franckreporter/Getty Images, p. 126 (man
running); Rocketclips, Inc./Shutterstock.com, p. 126 (doctor & patient); Eric
Audras/Getty Images, p. 154 (man driving); Andrey_Popov/Shutterstock.com,
p. 154 (hands on steering wheel); mimagephotography/Shutterstock.com,
p. 161 (woman); Hero Images Inc./Alamy Stock Photo, p. 165 (medical office
worker); Tony Tallec/Alamy Stock Photo, p. 165 (medical assistant); Maridav/
Shutterstock.com, p. 168 (woman thinking); Tiko Aramyan/Shutterstock.com,
p. 168 (to do list); Thinkstock Images/Getty Images, p. 169 (man).